Ancestor Reverence & Ritual

A Beginner's Guidebook on Honoring
Those Who Have Come Before

Rev. Mignon Grayson
Sacred Mysteries World Wide, LLC

Ancestor Reverence & Ritual

A Beginner's Guidebook on Honoring Those Who Have Come Before

Kindle Edition

Rev. Mignon Grayson

Copyright © 2020
United States Copyright Office

DEDICATION

This book is dedicated to Olodumare / Ntr / God, my tutelary Orisha Eshu, my Ancestors, my Spirit Guides, my spiritual Elders, and to Onile (earth) for the life and inspiration that flows through me. This book is a gift from them. May I always continue to receive their blessings as I walk upon this earth.

This book is also dedicated to You, the Reader. May you discover the beauty, uniqueness and power of your Spirit and realize your ultimate potential and find peace and balance through connecting with your honored Ancestors. They have been working behind the scenes waiting for the day you will recognize and honor them. They rejoice that you are taking this step to learn.

ANCESTOR INVOCATION

Ancestors near, we call to you.

Ancestors far, we call to you.

Ancient Ones who have escaped the wheel of incarnation,

We call to you.

Ancestors that sit at the feet of God in counsel.

We call to you.

We remember you.

We remember to call your names.

We remember to tell your stories to our young,

So that your memory is carried in our blood & hearts forever.

We ask for your guidance to direct us.

We ask for your wisdom to light our paths.

We ask that your love protects us as we move through this world.

Honored Ancestors,

Bring coolness to our homes, heads and life,

So that we will always know peace.

We praise you. We honor you.

Amen, Asé,

Maferefún Egun.

Honor to the Ancestors.

Special Thanks

This work would not be complete without mentioning the unending support and encouragement by some very special people in my life. First, my daughter, Tehja A. Fagains, whose vision of me I continue to hold and strive towards. She is my rock and my biggest encourager. She inspires me and is the reason I continue to move forward on my path. Her faith in my work keeps me grounded and on course. My big sister, Denise Phillips, who is always there to cheer me on, support and encourage me. She also helped me edit this work. She is one of the people I look up to most! A brilliant mind and a sweet spirit. My other big sister, Yvette Jackson, who is a light and love that is always there to nurture and lift me up.

I also am supremely thankful for the love and support of my spiritual sisterhood that surrounds me—Kathleen Bullock, who is my Spiritual Godmother, dear friend and Priestess of Oya. She inspires me through example and action of how love is always the ultimate reason for what we do in life and family, whether chosen or birth. Family is the vehicle of that love. Her love, guidance and support has helped me grow in so many ways. She also reminds me to always put my spiritual health as a priority. Gladys Wrenick who is my god sister and dear friend who, countless times, has been a source of wisdom and insight. Amy Fabrikant, whom I can always count on for love, advice and understanding. She reminds me to see a greater side of myself that often times, I forget. Last but certainly not least, my Coach and Mentor, Abiola Abrams, who continuously, guides, inspires and challenges me to discover my best self and to translate that part of me to those whose lives I touch. Her spiritual and business tools are incomparable! Her spirit is love and beauty in action.

The Goal of this Book

The goal of this book is to present to the reader various methods and tools to implement Ancestor reverence practices in their spiritual lives. Ancestral Reverence practices are world-wide and vary greatly not only by country, but by city, region, spiritual houses and neighborhoods. The best way to learn ancestral veneration is through an elder (someone who has been doing it significantly longer than you) imparting their knowledge person-to-person. That is the way this information is usually handed down in these traditions. It ensures not only that the steps and methods are transferred but also the heart and tone are communicated as well. It mirrors the ways of ancestral honoring by learning from elders. Ancestor veneration is more than a system of a ritual actions. It embodies the historical soul of a family. However, in the age of technology and the inability of many to find reputable guidance in their respective localities, a guidebook to get started is helpful. This book in no way replaces direct guidance from an elder. I recommend finding a Priestess or Spiritualist to learn from.

In order to understand life, understanding death is important. Death completes and makes whole our soul's experience of existence. Viewing death as another version of existence will broaden, deepen and expand every other spiritual concept that you will ever learn.

I decided to write this guidebook because I have been witnessing, lately, the strong desire people have to understand and participate in Ancestor reverence. There seems to be an internal drive to connect to this knowledge. As a result of this drive, I have also seen misinformation being given out as "fact." It is important to dispel the misinformation by providing information that has been passed down. When traditions are passed down from generation to generation, they have been time-tested by the communities in which they are practiced. Traditions connect people to the ways and wisdom of antiquity. Ancestor veneration is ancient. It signifies the human ability to connect spiritually with those who have departed the physical life thereby bringing a better understanding to the endless cycle of life.

This book is written to help those who would like to get started navigating the wide terrain of information out there. There are basic do's and don'ts that need to be known and adhered to. But mostly the Ancestor reverence techniques discussed in this book are not as structured as the rituals and rites associated with honoring divinities such as Orisha, Loa, Neteru, Abosum, etc. There is much room left for flexibility and creativity.

If you are looking for a book that brings a scholarly or intellectual viewpoint, this is not the book for you. This book is from the heart and soul of my own personal ancestral spirituality. This work is from an indigenous woman who answered an ancestral call to realign with and ignite from within the spirituality of her foremothers and forefathers. This is the perspective you will get from this book. This is my experience that I offer you within these pages.

It is my hope that this book gives the reader enough information to feel confident and informed enough to start and/or further develop their Ancestor reverence practice. Building a strong bond with your Ancestors will also help you to connect with your Higher Self and own your personal power more profoundly. The experience is emotionally and mentally nurturing and will help you to elevate your consciousness and grow spiritually. The Ancestors will guide and protect you along the way.

Blessings on your journey!

Contents

1

Introduction

Ancestor awareness is a growing movement and progressing to the center stage of focus in the spiritual healing arena in the United States. It is becoming more and more apparent across spiritual disciplines that there is a need for Ancestral reconnection and healing of Ancestral wounds. History tells us so. There is substantial evidence that connecting to ancestral heritage is foundational to spiritual development and is supportive of holistic spirituality. Ancestral reverence presents to us the unending cycle of life. This is not a unique perspective. Ancestor Reverence is very ancient and has been a core component of indigenous practices around the world for thousands of years. Ancient people understood the continuity of life through birth, death and rebirth. It was evidenced in nature all around. Seeing themselves as part of nature, part of the Creator, they could see their lives following the same cycle of birth-death-rebirth. Being in tune with nature is also being in tune with Spirit, they were able to hear the whispers of the voices of family members from across the veil between life and death encouraging them to delve deeper into ways to strengthen the bridge between worlds to receive messages from their Ancestors more clearly. For people who walk within the indigenous knowing field—that place of healing and knowledge accessed for millennia by ancient and current Native healers throughout the globe—Ancestral connection is an ordinary part of life.

Six million years of human life on the planet. Ancestors date back to the very beginning. This means we all come from a long line of people who were born on this earth, lived and then died and then reborn. This cycle of life has brought us to this very point in time and will continue into eternity. Ancestral reverence and connection taps directly into the collective and familial wisdom and knowledge of all the ages of the human experience on this planet – confirming the African proverb, *"...we stand on the shoulders of our ancestors."*

Ancestral reverence is founded on the belief that when the body dies, the spirit does not. The spirit is viewed as eternal and subject to many incarnations. Those Ancestors who have crossed over have only shed their physical bodies but continue to live on in the spirit realm. Ancestors are connected to the living by DNA which ties them to their descendants and to future generations. Because of their connection and love, they are interested in helping and intervening on their family's behalf to bring about positive occurrences. It is also a responsibility that is bestowed upon the Ancestors by the Divine. This is the part of the Circle of Life. The Ancestors utilize the advantage that they no longer have the limitation of their physical bodies and can go about the physical and spiritual world as needed to influence matters according to need, desire and the destinies of their descendants.

Ancestral reverence seeks to acknowledge and harness the collective wisdom of those that have gone before in order to gain balance and progress in life. Ancestors work to help us through life's challenges. They can also help us in our quest for spiritual evolution by acting as Spirit Guides or Tutelary Spirits.

The desire to communicate with our Ancestors is an innate part of the human experience. This is exhibited in the many forms of Ancestor reverence across nations globally. At some point, people think about their deceased loved ones and long to be able to speak with them again. We intuitively sense their presence in our wisdom bodies (physical and energetic), and it begs the question: how can we communicate with them? How can we hear their words of wisdom or comfort just one more time?

Our Ancestors are always around us ready to assist us. They are just a whisper away. They are constantly helping and encouraging us in our movement forward. When we get very still and meditate, they can send messages to us in the form of words, sounds, pictures or feelings. They often come in the form of inspirational thoughts that come to us and feel "true" or "accurate" or "certain." This type of communication shines through our awareness with pristine clarity. The Ancestors' continued guidance through the veil of death, is evidence of the endless circle of love that exists for each and every one of us. Reaching back through the Ancestral realm to the physical realm is no small feat. It takes tremendous energy, focus and dedication.

It is important that with the growing popularity of Ancestor reverence, that this ancient and sacred practice be held with the reverent treatment it deserves. Oftentimes in mainstream popular spiritual communities, the essence of time-honored traditions gets pushed to the side and the sensational aspects of a tradition become the main focus. People claim to be knowledgeable or expert on the subject with little experience. People think that when it is "spiritual" one has license to interpret and redevelop the systems in their own way that have been in place for eons. Ancestral reverence is traditional. It is Ancestral which means it was passed down in the communities and families over thousands of years. It would be wise to learn from elders so that the essence of the tradition can remain as intact as possible. It is the essence of the practice along with the heart that are most important.

When I began my journey reclaiming my ancient African and Native American spiritual practices, much of the advice from the Spiritual Elders I sat down with was to connect with and honor my Ancestors. In various divinations over time and in ritual directly from the mouth of Spirit, I have been told that my path is strong in Ancestral work or that "I am a daughter of Egun (the dead.)" As ominous as it sounds, it simply means the Ancestors are close to me. The source of my spiritual work would primarily come by way of Ancestral veneration. I became an Ancestral Medium quite by surprise at a ritual. An Ancestor appeared to me, that I allowed to speak through me to assist in helping the ritual participants. Since then, I have worked with the Ancestors in this manner off and on through the years, usually in ceremony and sometimes outside of it when an Ancestor arrives to help in an emergency or special situation. When walking this spiritual path, harmonizing the differences between indigenous culture and dominant society has been challenging. In some societies it is so natural, but in western society it is not.

Honoring my Ancestors has been a significant part of my spiritual life since the 1970s. I have been around the custom since a child. I remember going to West African Akan and Yoruba ceremonies in New York City where I grew up. My mother took me to at least one ceremony. She also came home one day with a set of elekes (spiritually consecrated beaded necklaces.) I was also brought to ceremonies by other adults in my life. African-based spiritual traditions have at the core of their theology Ancestor reverence. Asian-based traditions also have Ancestor reverence as an important part of how they honor the Divine. The blessings of the Ancestors are extremely important to them.

After my grandmother passed, my mother honored her mother with an altar- like setup. I don't believe it was an intentional altar, but something she felt drawn to do to continue to feel the presence of her mother. My grandmother was called "Mama" by both her children and grandchildren. My mother took a beautifully framed photo with Mama's picture and set it on top of the baby grand piano, graced with two elaborately ornate iron taper candle holders on either side of the framed photo. She would add fresh flowers from time to time. My mother also honored her mother in the way she spoke of her with such love and admiration. The stories she would also tell of Mama after her passing made us even closer to our grandmother. My mother also honored her grandmother in similar fashion. She made sure we at least knew her name and what she looked like. I remember when she refurbished and beautifully framed a photo of my great grandmother. The large photo was set in an ornate gold frame

13

trimmed in red velvet. I remember being amazed that I was related to the woman in the picture who was dressed old-fashioned like in the black and white movies I watched as a child! This is a simple form of honoring one's Ancestors. I'm still not sure if this is something my mother did instinctively, or she was advised to do by her association with African Traditional Religion. It seemed very natural to her. In her so doing, she nurtured my connection to my deceased relatives making my honoring of them an easy addition to my spiritual life once I was introduced to it. Ancestor Reverence is an integral part of my every day. When I wake up in the morning, the first thing I do is thank Olodumare (God), Ori (personal spark of the divine), Orisha (divinities), and my Ancestors. I have shrine in my home dedicated to them which I salute daily.

The perspective from which I write this guide on Ancestor reverence is that of a devotee of the Lucumi of Cuba and Isese of South West Nigeria Orisha traditions, as well as from the perspective of an initiate in the Palo Mayombe tradition of the Congo. My experience in this arena has been under the tutelage of different Priestesses & Priests of both Lucumi and Isese paths. My devotion to my traditions is a way of life. The methods that I share are from these traditions as well as some practices from other traditions acquired along the way. However, the major influence of the practices described in this book are from the Yoruba and Congo descended people as practiced in the Diaspora. This is what I learned from my elders and what I learned from my Ancestors through my connection to them. This is my experience as a devotee from a devotee's viewpoint. I share this so that you can begin your own unique and beautiful journey with your Ancestors.

You don't have to be a devotee of these traditions in order to honor your Ancestors. Every ancient people on the planet had some form of Ancestor reverence. I encourage you to discover the way your Ancestors honored their Ancestors during their time. Something extraordinary happens when we embrace our ancient ways of honoring Ancestors and other aspects of our spiritual history. It is a coming home. Your Ancestors rejoice.

Rituals presented within these pages may be used as an individual or in a group setting, or even be experienced in meditation if you feel drawn to that. In Ancestor reverence you can follow your soul, and your Ancestors will walk with you in the rituals and sit with you in the meditations and answer the call when libation is poured in honor of them. It is your birthright as a descendant of those who walked easily in the spiritual indigenous way. It is your birthright as a descendant of those Ancestors who stand ready and willing to uplift their family still living on earth.

2

Ancestors, Who Are They?

What exactly is an Ancestor as it relates to you directly?

An Ancestor is a blood relative that was an elder to us during our lifetime and also those that lived and died before we were born. We may or may not have known them directly. They are the souls of family members who are no longer incarnated. This is consistent with the widespread belief that humans have at least two parts—a physical body and some kind of non-physical spirit. The spirit portion is generally believed to be freed from the body by death and continues to exist in another realm. Ancestral spirits are often seen as retaining an active interest and even membership in their family and society. However, just like in life, in death there are categories of Ancestors. Two of them are the honored and *not* honored. The main focus of this discussion will be on the honored Ancestors.

An honored Ancestor can be qualified by the following criteria, (1) lived until adulthood; (2) was a positive, contributing member of society at the time of death, (3) non-hardened criminal at time of death, (4) mentally sane (without severe mental illness). This criteria are important to be able to identify the Ancestors who will be called upon to help you. The goal is to reap the beneficial contributions from our family's past to support and influence our present. When there are deceased relatives that did not live a life that contributed positively to society or directly to the family, there are specific measures to take in order to heal that part of the ancestral heritage. There is an erroneous belief that your ancestors immediately transform into enlightened and elevated beings upon transitioning to the afterlife. Although each person is unique in their purpose and destiny, this is not true as a whole. When a person passes on, they take with them the energy of the lifetime that was just departed including their mental and emotional states. It is up to the spirit to recognize that they have to shed this in the afterlife in order to develop. Because it was the physical world that was left behind, the shedding of the physical experience and limitations occurs upon death. The Ancestor can immediately be free from illness and debilitation of the body. Especially if they accept they no longer have a physical body. It is not the same for the emotional/mental state. Emotional and mindset in the spiritual realm are magnified. The emotions and mindset directly relate to the type of character the person expressed and maintained throughout their life. This is not as easily shed upon death.

In the land of the Ancestors, existence continues for each spirit. They are interacting with each other and, going about their roles and responsibilities, but somewhat differently than here. One very important responsibility they are charged with is to assist their loved ones on Earth.

(On the cover, Anna Douglas Ayers. My maternal Great Grandmother)

Ancestors are our spiritual foundation without a doubt. Before any angel, archangel, orisha, goddess/god, divinity, etc., it is our Ancestors who have our backs and look out for us all of the time. Needless to say, we are who we are because of them deciding to bring children into the world, and because of their survival, sacrifices, triumphs and struggles. When they leave this earthly life, they leave their earthly concerns and struggles behind, but they do not forget about us because they are connected to us and remember how life was for them. They, like most parents, want us to elevate, be happy and to achieve our highest destinies. The following information is a combination of what I have learned and practiced, along with my own observations and thoughts regarding the realm of Ancestors and Ancestor Reverence. This is by no means an authoritative viewpoint. There are many different beliefs and Ancestor practices worldwide. Each are different and beautiful within the context of the cultures from which they were birthed. The realm of Spirit isn't exact, finite, or controlled by us. We are constant explorers continuing to discover the vastness of the non-physical realm. The viewpoints and practices of Ancestor Reverence are as diverse as the ethnic groups on the planet. No one culture has the end-all-be-all perspective. No one person is the one and only exalted authority. All you can really rely on once you've received guidance from Elders who have practiced Ancestor Reverence, is your own personal, intimate experience as you begin to revere your ancestors and strengthen your relationship with them.

My personal experience has been one filled with love, comfort and wonderment. It never ceases to amaze me how my Ancestors answer my prayers. They also see beyond our time and space and avert harmful situations. One thing to understand about Ancestral reverence is energy in equals energy out. Meaning, the reverence we pay them is an energetic force that they receive. They in turn return that energy to you in the form of assistance and guidance. The energy they return is magnified by the essence of the spirit realm. What you gave them is returned at least 100-fold. Even though the Ancestors are already involved in their assignment to assist without you doing anything, you doing your part makes them that much for effective in what they are able to do for you.

Egungun – Collective Ancestral Spirits

In Nigeria there is practice of Ancestor veneration known as Egungun. The concept of Egungun is that there are Ancestral spirits who visit through the preparation of special community-wide ceremonies. These particular Ancestral spirits represent the collective Ancestral realm of spirits all the way back to antiquity. The ceremonies invite these powerful Spirits to come and bless the community with prosperity, healing and success in all endeavors, not just for individuals but for the community as a whole. Not much is known about these rites, due to immense secrecy. The Egungun society is responsible for the sacred rituals and ceremonies of Egungun Masquerade. This society holds its rites under extreme secrecy. You can only access this if you are initiated into the Egungun Society. The Egungun festivals are held regularly to venerate the Ancestors for the whole community. It is a large undertaking with many ritual applications. When the Egungun Festival happens, people travel far and wide to be able to participate in hopes of receiving messages from their Ancestors.

From the site, https://africa.si.edu/exhibits/resonance/44.html

"Egungun is a visible manifestation of the spirits of departed Ancestors who periodically revisit the human community for remembrance, celebration, and blessings. It is a unique cultural tradition practiced by the Yoruba of West Africa and their descendants in the African Diaspora, particularly in Brazil, Cuba, the Dominican Republic, Barbados, and the United States. These spirits constantly bless, protect, warn, and punish their earthly relatives depending on how their relatives neglect or honor them."

A Special Note about Children Who Pass Away:

Many parents, unfortunately, have had children die young that never reached adulthood in their incarnation. This is the most painful experience a parent can ever know. My deepest condolences are with the parents of the world who know this type of pain and loss. Trust that although your child preceded you in death, know that the spirit of the child holds a special position in your spiritual system of Ancestors. This time around they are not considered Ancestors who guide the whole family, but they are your direct loving guidance and protection. Child spirits come to visit parents and siblings to give support and to comfort them letting them know they are okay, and that they are near and not to worry about them.

A Viewpoint of Ancestor Groups

I think of Ancestors in groups. There is the family group connected to you by DNA. The family group extends to include people that have come to be family to you during their lifetime that do not share DNA. Their close bond with you creates a strong connection. I like to call this "spiritual DNA." There are schools of thought that only your blood Ancestors should be included, but several of my elders do not follow this rule. Neither do I. Then, the next group would be our community or shared Ancestors. They are the deceased whom because of their work on behalf of large groups of people while they were living on earth are connected, remembered and revered by that larger group or community, and lastly, there are the Ancestors who are responsible for the well-being of particular ethnic groups although DNA may not be direct, there is spiritual tie because of the ethnic grouping. I like to call this the **Ancestral Ethnic Pool**. The Ancestors can be members of one or all of the groups.

Although, our existence isn't linear, our minds have been trained to perceive existence in linear time. In this regard, we can acknowledge our Ancestors by their generational timeline. A generation is considered roughly 30 years. Your most recent Ancestors can be classed in the range of 1-20 generations prior to you; older Ancestors are in the 21-40 generations prior; and even farther back are your ancient Ancestors in the approximate range of 41+ generations prior to your birth.

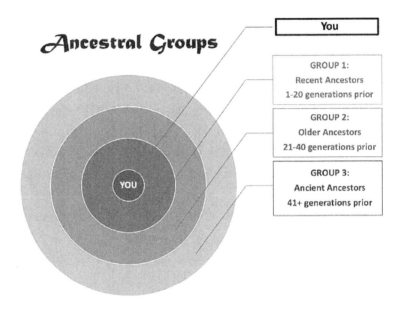

Most of us can't go beyond 5 generations back when it comes to naming our Ancestors and knowing their stories. Going farther and farther back, the names become more and more obscure. The stories become legends or fairytales. Even more so, our Ancestors become faceless, storiless, unknowns to us. The farther back we go in our family line, what were once personal and relatable people, become groups of unknown people and geographic locations. However, we cannot help but feel linked to them because we know of them to be family. We are told of our geographical origins, however specific or generic, which ties us to particular places in the world, particular times and particular histories.

Stages in the Afterlife

Another way to group Ancestors is in "length of time since becoming deceased." Once death occurs, there are stages that the spirit goes through as they move on to their afterlife experience or realm. For the purpose of this discussion, the categories have been broken down in the following way: recently deceased (10 years or less); deceased (11-30 years); and, long deceased (31+ years.) There is no official timeline that I know of. Actually, in the world of Spirit, timelines should be taken loosely. Time moves differently in that realm. However, in an effort to present ways of categorizing the Ancestors which frames the way we perceive them, and the Ancestral realm, the following breakdown is a perspective of the afterlife experience:

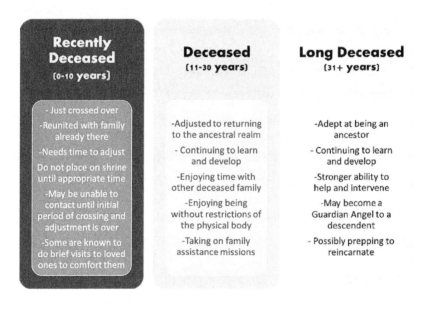

Recently Deceased
(0-10 years)

- Just crossed over
- Reunited with family already there
- Needs time to adjust
- Do not place on shrine until appropriate time
- May be unable to contact until initial period of crossing and adjustment is over
- Some are known to do brief visits to loved ones to comfort them

Deceased
(11-30 years)

- Adjusted to returning to the ancestral realm
- Continuing to learn and develop
- Enjoying time with other deceased family
- Enjoying being without restrictions of the physical body
- Taking on family assistance missions

Long Deceased
(31+ years)

- Adept at being an ancestor
- Continuing to learn and develop
- Stronger ability to help and intervene
- May become a Guardian Angel to a descendent
- Possibly prepping to reincarnate

Our more recent Ancestors: mother, father, grandparents, siblings, cousins, aunts, uncles, etc., are what most people are concerned about when starting on a path of Ancestor reverence. To connect again with those deceased whom we have had a bond with is a longing that is real and can weigh on our emotions. The void that the person left behind is tangible to those still living. They are missing their loved ones. It can be disruptive to mental and emotional peace. With Ancestor Reverence, we can build a bond with their non-corporeal energy signature and communicate with them either through divination or psychic connection.

The feeling of the void that she/he left can be lessened and their presence can be felt energetically. Sometimes they will show up in our dreams, or they will find ways in which to send signs that they are around. It can be in the form of a fragrance, a song, or numbers that are repetitive, flowers, animals… anything that you know represents them or for which they had a special appreciation. Another way they show up for us is when we have a strong sense of their presence.

There seems to be a general misconception in modern Abrahamic religious thought that once we are deceased, we have nothing to do. The deceased are usually said to "rest in peace." The truth is the Afterlife is just that… a non-physical LIFE. Ancestors are actively involved in different things. It's just in a different way, in another realm. Ancestors (and all spiritual beings) can show up on the earth plane to visit many people at the same time. It wouldn't be out of the ordinary for the children of someone who is deceased to all have the same strong feeling of their presence at the same time. They care very much for our well-being, success and fulfillment. That is why Ancestor Reverence includes asking them for assistance and guidance in everyday affairs. They want us to ask. They want to help us.

When we go farther back into our Ancestral lineage, there are Ancestors who have obtained a certain level of spiritual growth both through their work on earth and in the ancestral realm who are no longer required to incarnate. They can if they desire to take on a certain task to help humankind. They usually have lived many incarnations and learned their required lessons. However, they do still tend to their family members on earth but their strength and ability to assist has even more potency. That is why Ancestral reverence is also important. The reverence we give them aids in their growth and development during their time in the ancestral realm. Our reverence strengthens them energetically and gives them greater opportunities to continue their growth while in a non-physical form. Their work on our behalf is motivated by their love and caring, however, when they are able to help us it also elevates them. It is a relationship of reciprocity. The stronger and more elevated our Ancestors are, the stronger and more able they are to intervene on our behalf in our earthly lives and to assist in our endeavors.

Once you go extremely far back into your Ancestral line you will then be in the time of the Ancient Ancestors. It is believed that the Mystics, Priests, Shamans, Medicine People, etc. of many ancient and lost societies had reached high levels of spirituality and a profound connection to the Divine Creator. They were able to tap into Omniscience and develop and design spiritual systems to physically and spiritually heal and uplift the masses. These Ancestors aren't as easily accessed because of their different vibratory rate. They exist on the higher spiritual plane and if we ourselves are not at a certain vibratory rate, we may not be able to interact with them in a way that will result in beneficial understanding. If it is a goal of yours to connect with them, it's best to develop yourself spiritually and physically. There are times when the Ancients modify their frequency to interact regardless of where you are spiritually. So, a connection can happen if they choose. There can be very valuable and profound messages received should you experience a connection with an ancient Ancestor. Sometimes we are in need of a "jump-start" to help us to the next level in our development. That is what the ancients can provide.

Cycle of Life and Reincarnation

Reincarnation is when a person dies, and their spirit born back into the world at a later time. All of us are reincarnated spirits. Our Ancestors will be reincarnated at some point. When we die, the same will happen for us. When an Ancestor reincarnates, the spiritual essence of who they were in their last incarnation remains in the Ancestral realm. Their spirit reincarnates usually as a family member ready to begin their experience in the current timeline. The spirit of who they were remains in the Ancestral realm. That's why you can still give homage to an Ancestor and they can simultaneously be reincarnated. Spirit is not linear or singular, but a vast spiraling existence of the Creator.

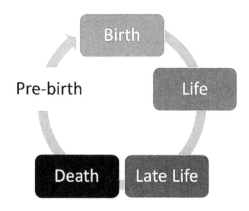

The cycle of birth-life-death and rebirth is an unending cycle reflected in all of life. The changes of seasons, the moon cycles, the animal and insect worlds, all reflect this. Humans go through the same cycle physically and spiritually. What is interesting to note is that, we also have a stage just before birth where much goes on. When an Ancestor prepares for re-entry into the human realm on earth, there is a pre-birth stage where agreements on life assignments, major events, life path and destiny are made. Many cultures believe that Ancestors return to the same family line over and over again. There are other beliefs that humans can change gender and ethnicity in each incarnation. I am of the belief that any and all of it can happen and that there are no "hard" rules where this is concerned. There can possibly be an alternating of reincarnating processes. You could incarnate into the same lineage for thousands of years and then choose to experience something different at another point of your existence. Possible? Perhaps. At the core of all of human beings is the same Creator and in essence we are spirit before we are anything else.

The recent emergence of interest in Ancestors and Ancestor Reverence is taking centerstage in many spiritual arenas in the last few years. Where descendants of black and brown people have retained or reclaimed the tradition of Ancestor Reverence across the world, Europeans are recently stepping into the practice by way of the systems established and maintained by Africans, African descendants, Asians and Native Americans. I encourage people to reach back into their lineage and discover their own Ancestors' form of Ancestor Reverence.

Ancestor Reverence is a much-needed part of spirituality for all people across the world. It can help to heal wounds and trauma from the near and distant past. For the African and Indigenous descended people in the diaspora it is an imperative that will help us reconnect beyond the trauma of colonization to link into the ancient wisdom of our Ancestors to heal. It has always been part of ancient peoples' culture and spirituality. However, in Europe it was ripped away from its culture and replaced with the Abrahamic religions. If you notice most of the Abrahamic traditions don't mention Ancestor reverence in and of itself. However, if you look at many of the practices within the religions you can recognize it. How do you think Abrahamic religions are passed down? From the elders to the next generation. Are any of these elders celebrated after death? Yes, many. That is a form of Ancestor Reverence. If there weren't any value in Ancestors, then we wouldn't mention them in any aspect of our society. We would just move on as if everything started from this point.

Beyond this book, if you're interested in Ancestor Reverence, find a reputable Priestess or Priest who can help guide you along your journey. I have been revering my Ancestors for decades. It is a path that is beautiful, mysterious, fun and satisfying. It completes my experience of life on this planet and connects me with the spirits of people who love and support me. In this way, I never feel alone or completely lost. They uplift me, even during times when I do not have the strength to lift myself.

3

Why Honor Them?

Honoring our Ancestors completes the experience of life by building a bridge between this physical realm and the spiritual realm. It fills out and completes the view of the life we are experiencing. As spiritual beings housed in a physical body, we are dominantly spiritual. Not having a connection to the spirit realm makes us imbalanced. Our view of our world and existence becomes limited and narrowed. Our understanding of who we are in the scheme of life is muted. When you understand the life/death/birth are all interconnected experiences in life, it opens up the possibilities of your unlimited potential. You begin to be able to connect with a deeper understanding of yourself as a Divine being manifested on this earth. Ancestor reverence is proof that life is unending. A cycle that continues. It brings understanding to the cycles inherent in existence on this earth plane.

In exploring and honoring our Ancestral legacy, it helps us understand family dynamics, patterns, characteristic, behaviors, motivations for choices and changes in family location, education, and vocation. All of these dynamics helped to shape a familial identity that passes down through the family line. They give us major clues to who we are and why we may have a predisposition for certain things. Spirit will reveal new information and confirm old information.

The everyday benefit is that we no longer feel alone. We have a whole army of Ancestors who came before us to call upon. The Ancestors we knew and that we miss we are able to call upon and communicate with. It softens the devastation of the loss of a loved one knowing they are continuing and that you will be able to once again connect with them. With the exception of our Ori (personal divine essence,) no Orisha has the depth of closeness that we have with our Ancestors.

29

When we strengthen our bond with our Ancestors, they are more able to help us and intervene on our behalf. They do it anyway, but having a stronger connection supports stronger and faster results in the manifestation of what it is you are requesting of them. Ancestors are your protectors who alert you of danger or make sure you avoid certain situations by turning you away or rerouting you. Ancestors block lower spirits who may try to come in contact with you. They setup an energetic barrier to the things that are not beneficial to you. Ancestors also bring comfort in times of adversity. They also bring blessings of wealth and prosperity.

We have thousands of Ancestors. Many have different talents. They were skilled or experts in different fields. When you are attempting to achieve something, you can sit down at your altar and ask for the Ancestors to step forward who have experience in this area to help you with understanding or achieving a certain skill level. For instance, if you have an Ancestor that was great at crafting wood, or excellent in business and you are endeavoring in either of those types of achievements, you can call on them specifically by name. If you don't know of anyone by name, you can also ask in general for any Ancestor to step forward who may have expertise or be able to help to step forward, they will answer you. Their answer maybe in the form of inspiration, whispers, the information falling into your lap out of the blue, or you meeting someone who can take you to the next level of what you're doing. Oftentimes Ancestors communicate in these more subtler ways than actually appearing before you and speaking to you. Although, this can happen too.

Ancestors represent love. The love of a mother. The love of a father. Grandmother love. Grandfather love. They also represent the stories of the ages that have passed that are rich with experience, excitement, incite and drama. Depending on how well you build your relationship, they will share their stories with you through direct conversations, images, or you will uncover history in documents, books or from other relatives. You will be led to where the stories are held. Having their love surround us and their stories within us gives of the security of being held in grace-in-action. You are never completely alone. Ultimately, our goals with our Ancestors are for balance, harmony, happiness, protection, healing, and strengthening both spiritually and physically.

Please note: Ancestor Reverence practices call on the elevated and honored Ancestors only. Most of us have deceased people from our family that haven't made it yet to the honored status due to their lower state of expression. Those Ancestors are not allowed to commune with you as they don't have anything valuable to offer just yet. Sometimes they are drawn to you if you have decided to walk a path to grow spiritually. Your light is attractive to those who have passed who recognize they need the light. Should they get around the protections you have and hang onto you, assistance should be sought to help them detach and move on. There are things that you can do, but I would not recommend them without knowing where you are spiritually and how strong your protections are. If you feel you have a spiritual attachment that is not healthy, seek help from an experienced and reputable Priestess or spiritual practitioner.

Also, unelevated Ancestors (earthbound spirits) can also be attracted to your darkness. The ones that refuse to move on and stay trapped near the earthly realm seek to continue to experience life through those still living by attaching themselves to someone who is spiritually weak and unhealthy and whose defenses are practically non-existence. This phenomena can be a root cause of some spiritual problems and blockages.

Not all blockages are signs of an unhealthy spirit connection. It can also be that there are some things that are needed by the Ancestors in order for you to move forward. Again, this is determined by an investigation through divination by a reputable Priestess.

4

Ways to Honor Ancestors

Remembrance, Prayers, Altar, Ritual, Offerings, Feast / Food

The most simple way to honor your Ancestors is by remembering them. They are pleased by you saying their names and telling their stories, especially to the younger generations. Putting on their favorite music, reading poetry or passages from their favorite books at the altar are appreciated by them. Lighting a candle for their birthdays or death days as they come up also honors them through remembering them.

Some of the other ways to connect with the Ancestors are through ritual (prayer, libation, altar setup), sacred song, rhythm and movement. Ritual creates an energetic container that invites and welcomes the Ancestors. An altar setup is central in ancestral connection as it provides a physical space in your home that becomes a portal – a doorway -- that has a "welcome mat" inviting the Ancestors to visit. The Ancestors desire to help and love to visit those of us who are still living our day-to-day lives. Prayers help to make our Ancestors stronger on their continued spiritual journey. It elevates them as well as ourselves. Incorporating prayer is important in ancestral communication as it elevates the energy connection. Most of us enjoy music and dancing of one sort or another. Our Ancestors still enjoy the same. When we sing songs to them and dance in their honor it is another form of communication, welcoming and inviting them to join us in the good feelings that music and dance bring. Drumming, in particular, has been used since ancient times to call the spirits. Certain patterns create an energetic beacon that calls to the Ancestral spirits and brings them to the gathering.

Prayers to the Ancestors

Here are a couple of prayers that you can use in your Ancestor reverence practices. They are generic and can be used across the spiritual spectrum. You will notice within the prayers there is a combination of praise and uplifting, acknowledgement, and a request. Many of us are raised that we shouldn't ask for much. We are taught humility to a fault. Our Ancestors come to us to help us. That is their role and responsibility. There is every reason to ask them for help.

Ancestral Invocation Prayer

Elevated Ancestors,
It is I, (YOUR NAME) who is the daughter/son of (YOUR MOTHER'S NAME) call upon you to be with me in this moment.
I ask for you to guide me in life and assist me with my endeavors.
I am your descendent, the continuation of your hopes and dreams
Your blood is my blood, my DNA is the same
I feel you in my bones. I am you and you are me.
I show my heart to you. I share my pains with you.
I share my joys with you. So that you will be proud and at peace
Please grant me the power to achieve (STATE YOUR REQUEST)
Always grant me health, wealth success prosperity
So that I may be strong enough to honor and grow your legacy.
I have not forgotten my commitment to our lineage,
and I vow to never forget. Thank you.

Divine Light Ancestor Prayer

I call on light from the Divine
I give light to my spiritual guides,
Guardian angels and protector spirits.
I give light to my Ancestors so

that they may guide me by providing light
where there seems to be darkness
so that I may clearly be directed
down my destined path.
I now walk peacefully down the path
hand in hand with the divine
and all those who guide me in
tranquility and love. I now hear clearly
as to my purpose, plan and objective
for this moment and for my lifetime.
I now see clearly as light shines within me
leading me toward prosperity, abundance,
progress, and evolution.
And so it is. And so I am guided.

Prayer to Our Most Ancient Ancestors

Most Ancient Ones, I call back through the vast reaches of time to you!
Back through recorded history, before the Nubians built their pyramid
temples.
Before the Romans fought and fell, City, Republic and Empire
Before the fertile lands between the Euphrates and the Tigris were
cultivated and cultures rich and vast sprang up.
Before the great cataclysm that shook the earth.
Before the land bridge to the Americas was crossed.
Before all these things you were there.
We do not forget you this day, most Ancient Ones.
You are us, and we are you, our DNA the same as yours.
Your minds bright and shining, your words wise, your hands building for
the future just as ours.
We thank you for your gifts and we thank you for your survival. We are
you, come back again, building on your work through the shifting sands of
time. Most Ancient Ones, please accept our (prayers and/or) offerings!

Libation

In many African indigenous practices, libation is a way to honor the spirits with the pouring of water (sometimes liquor) on the ground or into a receptacle while praying in a particular way that honors the Divine, nature, high spirits and calls upon the Ancestors in a particular order. This ritual is designed to open a portal that attracts the Ancestors to the space/time of where the ritual is taking place to commune and bless those in attendance.

Pouring Libation

The following is a generic libation prayer. Libations are usually done in the native language of the culture of origin. Most popular would be in the Yoruba language of the people of the southwest Nigeria. To simplify things, I'm sharing a libation prayer in Yoruba with English translation that can be used for people who are just getting started. The process is to first call upon the freshness and coolness which water brings and then proceed with the prayer pouring a dash of water into the earth or into a vessel.

Pouring of libation is a good idea upon setting up your Ancestor altar. It is also good at the start of your day or every few days.

You will notice in the Yoruba prayers the mentioning of "coolness" The concept of "coolness" is akin to balance. Coolness is not too hot or cold. It is a balanced and peaceful state from which action can be taken in any direction needed. Maintaining (or returning to) coolness allows clear and calm thinking.

Technique:

When pouring libation indoors. Have a cup or glass and a bowl. Fill the cup/glass with cool water. I like to blow into the water and say "ashe." Make sure the water is room temperature or cold (do not use hot water, it agitates.) Also, make sure you have enough water in the cup to last for the entire libation. You should not need to refill the cup in the middle of the prayer. Hold the cup of water above the bowl. At the end of each sentence splash a little water into the bowl from the cup. Using only the English translation is perfectly fine. However, if you decide to try the Yoruba words, definitely follow with the English translation to ensure the spirits understand what you are saying in case you mispronounce any words.

Libation Prayer

OMI TUTU
(May the water be cool and refreshed)
ONA TUTU
(may the road be cool and refreshed)
ILE TUTU
(May the house; the home be cool be cool and refreshed)
TUTU LAROYE
(May a calm messenger proceed all our prayers)
OLODUMARE AJUBA IKU MBELESE
(God I (WE) give homage, I (WE) salute the Ancestors that sit at your feet) MOPEO *(I call you)* ASE *(So be it)*
MOJUBA OLODUMARE, IBAYE BAYE TONU
(We give praise to the Owner of existence)
MOPEO *(I call you)* ASE *(So be it)*
IBASE OLOJO ONI
(I call upon and give praise to the owner of this day)
MOPEO *(I call you)* ASE *(ashay)* *(So be it)*
MOJUBA ORI

MOJUBA GBO GBO IMALE
MOJUBA ORUNMILA ELERIN IPIN IBIKEJI OLODUMARE
(I call upon and give praise to Orunmila, the witness to all choice of destiny, second Orunmila. Second only to Olodumare, and Owner of 256 Odus)
MOJUBA ESU *(Eshu)*
(I Give Praise To Baba Esu. (Eshu), The Road Opener) MOPEO *(I Call You)* ASE *(ashay) (So Be It)*
MOPEO *(I Call You)* ASE *(ashay) (So Be It)*
MOJUBA *GBO GBO* ORISA *(Orisha)*
MOPEO *(I Call You)* ASE *(ashay) (So Be It)*
MOJUBA GBOGBO EGUN WA
(I Call Upon and Give Praise to All the Ancestors of Good Character)
MOPEO *(I Call You)* ASE *(ashay) (So Be It)*
MOJUBA (INSERT ANCESTOR NAME)
MOJUBA (INSERT ANCESTOR NAME…continue until you have said everyone you intend)
IBASE *(Ibashay)* OMO AIYE
(I Call Upon and Give Praise to The All The Children Of The World)
MOPEO *(I Call You)* ASE *(ashay) (So Be It)*
IBASE *(Ibashay)* ONILE
(I Call Upon and Give Praise to The Earth That Which Supports Us, The Ancestors That Supports Us When We Walk This World)
MOPEO *(I Call You)* ASE *(ashay) (So Be It)*
IBASE *(Ibashay)* OLOKUN
(I Call Upon and Give Praise to Olokun, The Essence of All Things that Come from the Depths of the Sea)
MOPEO *(I Call You)* ASE *(ashay) (So Be It)*
IBASE IBASE IBASE (Eebashay, eebashay, eebashay)
ASE ASE ASE O *(ashay, ashay, ashay oh)*
(As I Pay Homage to the Ancestors May My Homage Be Confirmed by God)

37

(while saying the above pour all the remaining water out into the bowl until the cup is empty). After you're finished, you can take the collected water and pour into to a plant or the earth.

Libation Prayer #2 (short and sweet and English only)

Fresh water, fresh water, fresh water,
May Mother earth be cool and refreshed (pour a dash of water)
May our guiding spirits be cool and refreshed (pour a dash of water)
May our honored Ancestors be cool and refreshed (pour a dash of water)
I / We give praise to (Insert Ancestor Name) (pour a dash of water)
(REPEAT THE LINE ABOVE UNTIL YOU'VE SAID ALL THE ANCESTORS' NAMES)
May my (our) heads be cool and refreshed (pour a dash of water)
May our interactions be cool and refreshed (pour a dash of water)
May the day be cool and refreshed (pour a dash of water)
May our movement be cool and refreshed (pour a dash of water)
May my (our) loved ones be cool and refreshed (pour a dash of water)
May those who want to harm me be cool and refreshed (pour a dash of water)
May... (add any other thing, situation, event, etc. you want to bring coolness to)
May it be so! (3xs) (while pouring all the remaining water out into the bowl until the cup is empty)

Pouring libation can be done at different places for different reasons. If you feel like a particular area of your home or house needs lifting, you can pour libation there.

Different places libation can be poured
- the ground (out at a gathering)
- on to a shrine
- on the ground in front of a shrine
- at the doorstep to a building/home/house/ front door
- on to a living plant (earth)

- into a receptable which is on the floor symbolizing the ground
- on the street in front of a venue

General Offerings

Regular offerings to Ancestors are standard practice. Offerings can be given daily, weekly, monthly or quarterly. It is up to you and your family how to schedule Ancestor reverence. What is important is that once you begin, you continue. Devotion and regular interaction are central to successful relationship strengthening. Offerings can be as simple as cigar/tobacco smoke, liquor, a beverage, bouquet of flowers, prayers, letters, fruit, candles, favorite perfume/cologne, candy, pastries, burning sweet incense, playing music, placing a favorite item, handmade gifts, jewelry, etc. The way you would choose the items would be in line with what you know they enjoyed while they were alive. A personal item of an Ancestor placed on the altar is also a great way to remember and honor them. Make sure to replenish the perishable items weekly or remove them once they have aged.

Food Offerings to Your Ancestors

Giving food offerings to your Ancestors is another form of veneration that is very common and standard in Ancestor reverence. Food is either specifically prepared for them or you can make extra of what you are preparing for yourself and your family to give to them. This is a way of providing them with nourishment just like you would any other family member and loved ones. There are a few ways in which you can give an offering of food to your Ancestors. Understand that this is not a symbolic act. When you provide food to your Ancestors, they actually receive it and partake of it. Understanding the laws of spirit and the universe, is to understand we live in a duality. There is the physical realm and the spiritual realm. Consequently, all created reality has a spiritual component in the spiritual realm. The food that is provided to the Ancestors, once placed on the altar the spiritual counterpart of the food appears in the Ancestral realm. Same for the food that you offer that is not on an altar, when prayed over as an offering to them actualizes its spiritual component to be present in the spirit realm and becomes available to them in the spirit realm. Should you decide to offer food to your Ancestors you will notice how it decomposes differently than if you just left the food out unattended. The food offering to the Ancestors seems to crystalize and age, much, much slower if at all. I've also noticed that depending on the offering, the next day you can see that the essence of the food has been quickly taken by the Ancestors. When I see that, I know the food was a favorite and they thoroughly enjoyed it, so much so, that it went like hotcakes!

How to Give Food Offerings

If you do not have an altar/shrine, you can give a food offering by first making your plate of food and then take a small plate and put some from your plate onto it. They love when you share from your plate. It is a very personal and heartwarming gesture. Put the plate on the side in your kitchen saying a brief prayer and acknowledging this sharing straight from your plate is for them. Alternatively, you can take a bit of the food you've prepared straight from the pots onto a small plate (or large) and say a prayer over it. Let the Ancestors know that you are giving this to "all of your elevated Ancestors so they can be nourished in the spirit realm." Any prayer from your heart is quite fine. Leave it on the counter or place the plate as another setting where you are eating your meal. If you want to place a small tealight candle next to it you can, but it's not necessary. Let it sit for a few hours or overnight -- whatever fits your living situation. Discard into the garbage or in nature. Instead of at the table, the prepared plate of food can be placed on your Ancestor altar if you have one. You can do this whenever the mood hits you. Or, you can establish a regular routine the Ancestors can come to depend on.

If you have an altar/shrine one of the most easiest offerings of food to make is a bowl of assorted fruit. Buy a selection of different fruits and arrange them nicely into a bowl or on a plate and present it to your altar. What is great about having an altar., is it allows you to do large food offerings. For a large food offering for your Ancestors, you should plan ahead. Decide on some of their favorite foods and cook a beautiful meal. You can include beverages, desserts, etc. Light a white candle, play music and dance. What I usually do is plan in a way that the food I prepare is also food that my family and I can eat. That makes it a feast for us all.

After preparing the food, dish out a plate or two for your Ancestors of everything and put it on the shrine. Light the candle. Let them know you prepared this in their honor. Thank them for all that they do for you. Say an Ancestor evocation prayer and you can also pour libation in front of the altar. *(instructions in previous chapter).* This is definitely a time when I use my Ancestor staff to call upon my Ancestors by name. After placing the food on the altar, saying a prayer and/or pouring libation, I begin to hit my staff on the ground in front of the alter. With each hit I call one Ancestor by name repeating the name 3 times. This is to ensure they hear you. You are calling across into the spirit realm. Start with the Ancestors who are most recent and work your way back to the oldest. When you've run out of names then declare "I call the elevated Ancestors of my mother and father's side known and unknown." This will conclude the offering ritual. Then the rest of the family can eat. This large food offering can be done every month, every couple of months, or once in a while. This is yours to establish as you wish. It is an undertaking that needs time and energy. Prepare well in advance, get your rest the night before, and start early. You don't want to be exhausted and frustrated. You want to be in a calm, peaceful and joyful mood when taking this ritual step.

If you have children, this is a great way to make it fun for them. In my experience children love seeing the food go on the Ancestor shrine and ask questions about who, what, and why. This is a perfect way to teach them about honoring their Ancestors. For my children this practice has deepened their understanding of themselves as spiritual beings, they are very sensitive and respectful of the elderly and recognize the value of time spent with those we love while they are still alive.

Many of us have changed our eating habits and no longer eat as our parents and Ancestors did. When providing food to your Ancestors, you should be prepared to step out of your comfort zone and prepare what they would eat. I've heard some people who have become vegan/vegetarian say "it doesn't matter, they are spirits and will understand..." Yes and no. I would advise against pushing your eating style upon your Ancestors. Just like if you sat down to eat as a vegan and someone put a pork chop on your plate and said ... "well it's food, eat it." You wouldn't like it would you? Going out of your way to give the Ancestors what they like is a sign of love and respect. Of course, for the smaller day to day offerings from your pot or plate are fine, but if you prepare a whole meal just for them, make the food they like. If this is too hard for you, purchase prepared food and add something that you've prepared to the offering.

Strange Requests - Caution: If you experience an Ancestor requesting items from you such as drugs (illegal or prescription) or any other debilitating substance, you should immediately stop communicating with the Ancestor. This includes you having a strong urge to give this substance to them as well. You may feel it is something you decided upon. It is more than likely a strong request from a deceased relative to you. Do not give them any such thing. This deceased relative is not elevated and seeks to continue to live their earthly life by your hand or through you as an attached earth-bound spirit. Should this happen, I recommend immediately seeking a reputable Priestess to help you break this Ancestor's attachment to you and help to elevate them. Equally, if an Ancestor suggests you indulge in nefarious behaviors, illicit or illegal actions, immediately seek the help of a qualified Spiritualist. Low-level deceased family relatives are not to be entertained by any means. I do not include low-level deceased family relatives to be of the status of the elevated Ancestors. These earth-bound spirits can be encouraged to elevate, but that is for an experienced Priestess to guide in how to go about it. Each situation is different and has to be investigated and a determination has to be made on what steps to take.

To Salt or Not to Salt?

In some spiritual arenas there is a prohibition on adding salt when preparing the Ancestors' food. In other arenas, it is perfectly fine. The reason for the inclusion of salt is to prepare the food the same way as when they were alive. I personally know my father would not appreciate unsalted food! When we would prepare low sodium food when he was alive for my mother who had high-blood pressure, he would always ask for the salt! LOL. So, tend to agree with salting the food… preparing it as if they were going to join you at the dining table. Disclaimer: if you're under the tutelage of an Elder in the tradition, go with what they have prescribed. I do not want anyone to go against the teachings of their spiritual elders.

Formal Ancestor Feast

This particular food offering comes by way of a divination reading from a Priestess/Priest of an African Traditional Religion. I'm sure there are others practices from across the world where this is prescribed to appease Ancestors as well. Should this be a determination in a divination reading, it is usually your Ancestors stepping forward and requesting it from you. Yep, a straight request from them. The diviner will find out exactly what the Ancestors want and will guide, instruct and help you accomplish the offering. When this a huge feast is requested, it is usually to also benefit other family members and your community. It may require attendees, drummers and assistance from other officiating Priestesses. It may also require other ritual steps leading up to the day of the event. That is all determined in the reading. It is a huge, lavish celebration that will bring much blessings to the person who carries out the request.

Ancestor Money / Joss Paper

There has been a relatively recent emergence in the spiritual community of offering Ancestor money to the Ancestors. This popular practice has been borrowed from the ancient Asian spirituality which has been part of Ancestor offerings for ages. Although China is the origin, this practice is reminiscent of the Ancient Kemet (Egyptian) people of North Africa who would bury their Pharohs and other important people with tons of supplies which included food, ritual items, personal care items, and money so that they can have all that they need in the afterlife and wouldn't want for anything.

In many parts of Asia, the burning of spirit money provided the Ancestors the currency needed for their comfortable survival in the afterlife. The temples accommodate this practice by installing special areas with large furnaces where the worshippers can safely burn joss paper Ancestor money. The paper money is folded in a ritual manner which is important to the success of the ritual. This ritual folding allows the Ancestors to know that it is joss paper and it will provide extra blessings and good luck. Burning actual money is considered unlucky in Asian cultures. Folded into specific shapes brings great luck to the offering of joss paper to the Ancestors.

I love the concept of this. It makes sense to me. I wanted to include this in my Ancestor reverence practice. I learned from my spiritual elders to ask the spirits if they approve before assuming that a particular offering is what they want or need. In keeping with this teaching, I asked my Ancestors if they would like to receive Ancestor money to help them. They told me "no." I then proceeded to ask various different ways they may want to receive the money. They said "no." Needless to say, my

Ancestors do not need or want Ancestor money. I say this to say, it is always a good idea when borrowing from another culture to check with your Ancestors first. I use the Obi form of divination in order to do this. If you have a yes/no system of divination, you can use that form. It is the prayers that activate the oracle and call the particular spirits you want to talk with to speak. If you don't know how to use divination, then you have the option to rely on your intuition. Going by a trend is not necessarily to going to reap the benefits that someone else has reaped.

How to Burn Ancestor Money

You can find traditional Ancestor money on Amazon or by doing a web search for "Joss Paper," or "Ancestor Money." The amounts of each bill are usually exorbitantly large, like $10,000,000. This, I believe, is a dramatic way to ensure enough money lasts for as long as the Ancestor remains in the land of the Ancestors and to also ensure the ease in paying off financial depths not only from the last incarnation, but also from any other. It could also represent the type of lavish good luck the person would like to receive as a result of this tribute.

Take the joss paper. Cleanse it of unwanted energy (smudge.) It has come through many hands before it got to you. At your altar, light a candle. Go into a meditative state envisioning what it is you are about to do. Say a prayer to your Ancestors and let them know what you are doing and why. Then, using a fire-proof container (metal incense holder, pot, etc.) and begin to burn the money bill by bill focusing, praying and affirming what you want to happen for your Ancestors and for yourself. See the Ancestor money traveling to your Ancestors into their hands and feel their gratitude. You can dispose of the ashes by burying in the earth or releasing them into the wind.

5

Ancestral Contact & Connection

Meditation/Contemplation

Meditation is the practice of clearing your mind of thoughts to allow for Divine insight and inspiration. Contemplation is focusing on a particular thought or concept that would eventually awaken to a deeper understanding. Both allow for you to slow your pace, slow your thoughts and settle into an alpha, delta or theta brain activity to allow for a state of awareness that is open to spiritual messages from Ancestors, guides and other angelic beings.

By engaging in regular meditation and contemplation you condition your mind to be in connection with the spiritual realm. By doing so, you are open to messages in any form they show up. This is a great regular practice to heighten your awareness and be able to communicate with your Ancestors effectively.

Journeying

Well-known in the spiritual traditions of the Native people of the Americas, this spiritual practice involves going within to the inner realm through a particular time-tested process. This process allows you to travel to an inner realm (the underworld) where you can meet your spirit guides in the form of animals and your Ancestors face-to-face. In this realm you can engage with them and receive direct messages of healing. Journeying uses a particular music (drumming) in the background and/or guided meditation to assist in traveling to the inner spirit realm. You can locate Shamanic Journeying drumming on YouTube. See which ones call to you. You may also have local drumming circles being held near you. If you want to engage in this type of spiritual practice, attend a journeying drumming circle at least once to experience the format. It is a tradition that is passed down from elder to student.

Conversations/Talking

Sitting at your ancestral shrine weekly or frequently to talk to them about life, what's going on with you, your hopes, dreams and desires—just as you would with a confidant is a way to form a stronger bond. Pour your heart out to them. They will send energies of comfort and be inspired to move in ways that bring balance and peace to your reality. This is an intimate way of building a bond and relationship with them. Nothing formal. Nothing fancy. Make sure there is a point in your talking that you become silent and go within and listen for messages from them. It may come in the form of words, images or feelings. Sometimes I feel their energy of love and them surrounding me to comfort me.

Writing / Auto-Writing

In this form of communication, you can write a letter or a note to your Ancestors, read it to them at your shrine, and place it there. The letter can contain thoughts, wishes, dreams, requests, desires or just a "thanks." Read out loud to them anytime you're moved to read. This is another form of intimate communication. Also, you can try auto-writing with your Ancestors. This would involve getting into a trance state and praying at your altar. Have a notebook and pen/pencil in hand. Open to a blank page and have your pen in hand ready to write. It's not about thoughts as it is about feelings. Let your Ancestors know by speaking out loud to them that you are ready to receive any messages they have and write it down. Breathe deep. Relax. Wait and allow. Be open to allowing the energy to move your penned hand across the pages. Whatever comes out on the paper try to decipher words, pictures or symbols. They may turn out to mean something. If so, then you've discovered one of the unique ways to receive messages from your Ancestors.

The Ways They Contact You

Inspirations

When you've been trying to do something or to move in a particular direction, there may be times when a crystal-clear inspiration all of a sudden drops into your awareness that sheds light on everything. Out of the blue, a solution cuts through with brilliant clarity. It can probably be attributed to a helping message from Spirit, which is usually your Ancestors. They can send the message to you as a strong unshakable realization, symbols, feelings, images, and people to help. Thank them when this happens.

Whispers

Oftentimes, Ancestors communicate by whispers. These whispers are usually persistent gentle, and soft thoughts. When we are not tuned in to the spirit realm, we often are dismissive of these whispers. However, they will persist until you begin to pay attention. Once you start to pay attention you will realize there is a strong message to receive. It can insist you change the way you are doing something or change the timing or direction you are going in. This is your Ancestor nudging you away from danger or moving you into an advantageous encounter or situation.

Ancestors are also known to let you know when they would like to partake of your food. Yes, your food. Have you ever noticed that some days you keep dropping food on the floor for apparently no reason? It just keeps happening. This is usually your Ancestors letting you know they want some of your food. One day I was in the kitchen preparing food and then all of a sudden, I took a step and the food I had in hand flew out onto the floor. There was absolutely no motion on my part that this should have happened! LOL. Just prior, I had little small incidences of food falling to the floor. I didn't get the hint. They decided to give me a bigger sign. When the food went flying, I laughed to myself and then out loud said 'ok, I get it, you want some of this food." If you continue to drop food and eating utensils consistently within a small timeframe, most likely your ancestors want some. Put a little on a small plate and place on the shrine or on the counter and say, "this food offering is for my all my elevated Ancestors." I find this to be a funny and heartwarming way the Ancestors let us know they are around.

Ritual

Ancestor meditations or drumming rituals are places where the Ancestors are invited in ritual manner to join the participants in sacred community. When in this sacred communal setting with others on a spiritual path, Ancestors will come and provide signs and messages to the group that are picked up by those who have developed their psychic abilities. The messages are translated to the Medium during the ritual. The Medium in turn communicates the messages to the intended person.

Mediums

During drumming ceremonies and spiritual masses, prayers and songs are sung to invite and uplift the Ancestral spirits. There are usually a few Ancestral Mediums in attendance. These Mediums allow Ancestors to take over their body for a short time. The Ancestors come and speak directly to the attendees about life, healing and anything else that they deem is important for the attendees at that point in time. Also, the Ancestors through the Mediums often perform energetic and spiritual cleansings on some of the attendees. When I've witnessed this, the Mediums seem to go directly to the ailment a person has and either performs energy work or tells the participant the steps that are needed for their healing. This is without prior knowledge or even knowing the person whom they are working on. This lets you know it comes straight from the Ancestors.

Dreams

Dreams are one way for your Ancestors to communicate with you. Your conscious mind is at rest and your subconscious and astral body take center stage while you are sleeping. The astral plane is conducive to both the incarnated and the deceased spirits. Also, it's easier for the deceased to navigate to the dream world while you are sleeping and come through into your dreams. Ancestors will often try to visit you or send a message in a dream. They will come to you in your dreams as often as they can, but it might only happen occasionally. It takes major effort. Dream visitations are not to be mistaken for regular dreams about your Ancestors. If a dream feels as real as waking reality, it was probably your Ancestor visiting. Also, if you receive a message in the dream is also an indication they were in your dream.

Divination

A very important part of communicating with your Ancestors is through divination. This type of divination is performed and interpreted by an experienced Priestess/Priest. The first part of the consultation is a message from your Ancestors commenting on various situations in your life, causes and potential solutions. This message will also include instructions for necessary offerings, prayers, baths, gifts and items needed for you to realign yourself for success and happiness. The second part of the consultation is asking yes/no questions to your Ancestors. The diviner is experience and will interpret the answers. Lastly, the consultation will close with a final word from the Ancestors to you.

Obi: Yes/No Divination

Having an Ancestor shrine will give you a place to use the system of four cowries (Obi) for divination and will then be able to access the Ancestral Spirits who will speak through divination. If you are not trained in Obi divination, you can use another form of yes/no divination that you are trained in. The components of the divinatory process to ensure you follow are: (1) opening prayer, (2) calling on your elevated Ancestors to be present. This ensures you are speaking to the right spirits, (3) ask your questions in a manner that can be answered with a yes/no manner, (4) record your answers, and (5) give thanks, then close the reading with a closing prayer. You can ask them about anything, really. Some example of questions you can ask:

"Am I in ire (ee-ray) with you, Ancestors, in order for you to continue to help me achieve success in life?" If no, then ask "what do you need from me in order to be in ire?" (ask about each offering separately, i.e., flowers, candle, water, liquor, food, fruit, honey, palm oil, prayer, song. With the first "yes" Then ask, "once I give you (_____) will I then be in ire?" If you get a yes, give them that offering. You are done. If no, continue to ask for other things. For instance, yes to flowers... "once I give you flowers then will I be in ire..." "no." "Would you like me to light a candle?" Answer, "Yes." Question, "once I give you the flowers and candle, will I then be in ire?" Answer, "yes." Give them flowers and a candle. You are good.

Ire (ee-ray) is a Yoruba word that means "good fortune, blessing, good favor." I like to ask this question every so often to ensure I continue to be in alignment with them. Staying in alignment with them ensures they have no impediments to doing the work they need to do for you. Or that they aren't lacking particular energy from you in order to act on your behalf. Also for you to stay in their good favor. Other questions can be asked of them as well. Ensure it is worth their time. Frivolous questions are to be avoided.

Those are the main ways to communicate through divination with your Ancestors. They are many systems of divination that can be used. This realm of spirituality is very vast and diverse.

Spiritual Mass - White Table

A Spiritual Mass is a gathering of Priestesses and Priestesses-in-training in the diasporic tradition of Lukumi/Santeria and Spiritualists. Others can attend at the discretion of the host. The purpose is to help participants develop their intuitive abilities and connect with their Spirit Guides under the careful instruction of the more experienced Priestess. This gathering is very helpful in identifying and strengthening intuitive abilities. Important messages from Ancestral Guides and Spirits are also received for the participants. They are usually held in someone's home or in a small community room, actually anywhere there is enough space for people to gather. The Misa includes a spiritual cleansing for everyone. There is a set format of prayers that begin and end the gathering to elevate the place, participants and Ancestor Spirits. The "white table" is the center of mass that must include certain elements in the setup.

There are a couple of types of Spiritual Masses. One is for developing Priestesses and Spiritualists. Another is a larger one that is conducted for the community where those seeking messages and cleansings can come. The goal is for healing and progress for the community. The basic elements of each are the same. The Spiritual Mass for the community is known far and wide and is well attended with people seeking messages and healing from their Ancestral Spirits. This is where the Ancestral Mediums play an important role in being a vessel for the Ancestors to come and give healing to the community. The Ancestor uses the Medium's body to speak through and do the cleansing work. The Medium is still in control and at any point can step forward and take control. When the Ancestor has concluded their work, they depart. The Medium is back to her/his normal self. All the time the Ancestor through the Medium is attended to by other experienced Mediums and Priests who are not functioning as a host for the Ancestors. They keep watch and make sure all goes according to plan.

Drumming Ceremony

The requirement of an official drumming ceremony for the Ancestors is determined through either divination, or direct message from an Ancestral Medium while at a meditation or other spiritual gathering. If this is the case, the specifics to the event will be determined in consultation with a Diviner. The ritual items and what's needed for the ancestral altar at the ceremony will also be determined. For this type of ritual event, there are also standard ritual items that are to be included which are known by an experienced Priestess. They will help guide the entire process.

An Ancestral drumming ceremony is one of my favorite events to attend. For many hours a place is transformed into a vessel for the Ancestral spirits to come and commune with the community. Priestesses/Priests and those in training come early to ritually prepare the space. The necessary pre-ritual ceremonies to bless and transform the room into sacred space are performed in order to be in harmony with the intent of the drumming ceremony: to pay homage, give thanks and invite the Ancestors to join the community. This is where the Ancestral Mediums play a significant role. All elements of the ceremony are ancient rites handed down from generation to generation. These rites merge past and present to create an appropriate ceremonial vessel for all. People come from near and far to join in the festivities. A traditional libation is poured at the opening of the ceremony in order to pay homage to all the spirits. When the drumming begins, traditional songs are done in a specific order to also give proper homage and respect to the spirits. Then the sacred songs to call the Ancestors are played all throughout the rest of the ceremony. Everyone sings the songs in call and response style. One after another the Ancestors come through the Mediums. When they arrive, they dance, they heal, they give messages to those who are in attendance. Trust me they know who is showing up even before the people who host the event! The Ancestors love to party and celebrate! Most importantly they love to come to heal.

When the spirits descend there is a major shift in the energy of the room. The Ancestors arrive with their persona resonating from another time and place. Old, yet timeless. It is a deeply sacred and powerful energy that permeates throughout the place. It is a sight to behold and an experience that is full of love. The Ancestors come to visit their descendants longing to bring much needed healing and hope. When you are asked to host a drumming for your Ancestors, it is a labor of love that benefits you as well as your family and your community who are in attendance. It is a treasured gift of spirit and heart.

Songs & Dances

As mentioned previously, the Ancestors love to party so when you are in the mood play their music and dance, call out their names, bring the memory of them to your mind and the feelings of love you have for them. This is an enjoyable way to honor and celebrate them and to bring them close. There are specific songs in the Orisha tradition that honor the Ancestors. You can do a search online. Ella Andall is one artist that I recommend. She has a song called *"Egungun (Prayers to the Ancestors.)"* Another is Lazaro Ros, he has an album called *"Eggun,"* which means *Ancestors*.

Music, song, symbols and dance have always been spiritual mediums that bring about profound connection with the Divine on all levels. Art helps us transcend our intellect and links us to divine pathways between the physical and astral realms.

6

Ancestral Connection Tools

Altars & Shrines

One of the most common connection tools is to create an ancestral altar or shrine in your home. The creation of a shrine/altar is setting up a space for your Ancestors to reside. It's like creating an energetic "room" in your home. This room is always ready to receive them. They can stay as long as they want or can go back/forth between realms as needed. Setting up an altar or shrine acts as an energy a beacon for the Ancestors that you call upon and invite. It opens up the communication between worlds so that they can more easily reach you. The altar is a place where you will keep your sacred items, their favorite items and various symbols of nature. It is also a place where you can offer them food, drink, light, prayers, conversation, music, etc. Life is a duality. Whatever is visible in the physical world also has a spiritual counterpart in the spiritual realm. In consecrating an area in your home and setting up an Ancestor altar, you are able to provide them with the spiritual double of your offerings.

Simple Altar

If you are an absolute beginner, it might be best to start small and then go larger once you've become comfortable with contacting your Ancestors. Over time, the Ancestors will give you ideas about what they would like to have on the altar in addition to the foundational items. To setup this simple altar all you need is a glass of water filled to the brim, a white 7-day candle in the glass, and an occasional bouquet of flowers, a picture of a deceased loved one (or a group). *No living person should be in the picture.* If you don't have a picture you can use a list of names. This type of altar is small and can be setup anywhere it is fire safe. I would replace the water and candle weekly. Add flowers weekly, or whenever you feel inspired.

Identify an area to place your altar where it will be undisturbed but also accessible for you to sit and commune. If space is at a minimum the, setup the altar where you can. It will act as a symbol of love and devotion to them which also strengthens them and your connection. Heart matters over size. Begin the setup by spiritually cleansing the area with Florida Water or any other spiritual water, smudge with incense of frankincense/myrrh or frankincense by itself or any other smudging herb. Say a cleansing prayer *(see example under Ancestor Prayers)*. Set everything up. Then say an Ancestor invocation prayer *(see example in Ancestor Prayers chapter.)* You can call out your Ancestors' names (3x's each to make sure they hear you). Speak your intentions if you like. Sit quietly for a little while to welcome them and see if any images or information comes. Sometimes it will just be a feeling of peace or happy energy. This is because they are happy that you remember and honor them. The first time you might not hear or see anything. It's okay. It takes time to build a strong bridge between worlds.

(pic., Ancestral Shrine on the floor)

56

Ancestral Shrine

Whenever you're ready, you can build your own ancestral shrine in your home. This is a bit more elaborate than the simpler starter altar. All you need is either a tabletop or a corner on the floor of a room. The reason for making the altar on the floor is symbolic the of how the Yoruba people of Nigeria traditionally bury their Ancestors underneath their homes in the ground. Creating the shrine on the floor ensures the offerings and ritual items are nearby them physically.

The living room, kitchen, dining room, family room or hallway is preferable as a location of the altar. It is not recommended to have an ancestor altar in the bedroom. That is where you rest for the night. Ancestors become more active at night. You want to keep your bedroom as the place where all energy is at rest when you are at rest. However, if it is the only space you have, it will suffice for the time being. You will need the following items: Pictures of your Ancestors *(no living person can be in the photo)*. If you don't have pictures of your Ancestors, you can make a list of names and place the list on the altar. You will also need a representation of the elements -- glass of water, a candle, dish of earth or a rock or crystal, incense holder and incense or a feather, and fresh flowers. If you have any personal items from the deceased, you can also add them to the altar. If you want to put a cloth to cover the tabletop, you can. The standard color used is white, but some people use a multi-colored printed fabric as well. It is up to you. I would stay away from the color black. Black is extremely powerful and is used in certain magickal instances. It's not the most conducive color for the Ancestor altar. It is best to use colors that reflect or symbolize light. Arrange the items on the altar in a way that is pleasing to the eye. Keep it neat and uncluttered.

Begin the setup by cleansing the area both physically and spiritually the same as mentioned previously. Clean the surface, then sprinkle or wipe with Florida Water or holy water. Once you've cleansed the area and setup everything, bless the altar and say a prayer to invite the Ancestors. This will complete the setup. If constructing your altar on the floor it is not necessary to have a cloth. An example of a prayer that can be used is:

Ancestor Prayer

Elevated Ancestors, I honor you
Spirits of my mothers and fathers, I call to you,
and welcome you to join me (for this moment.)
You watch over me always,
protecting and guiding me,
and in this moment, I thank you.
Your blood runs in my veins,
your spirit is in my heart,
your memories are in my soul.
*[If you wish, you may want to recite your genealogy here. This can
include both your blood family, and your spiritual one.]*
With the gift of remembrance.
I remember all of you.
You are dead but never forgotten,
and you live on within me,
and within those who are yet to come
I send you blessings of light
I send you blessings of love
Amen. So, mote it be.

You can always speak from your heart to the Ancestors. Any prayer that you are comfortable with or you know that they liked when they were living is also appropriate. Many Ancestors were Christians and reciting some of their favorite biblical passages would be appropriated by them. If you don't know what the favorite may have been, then using some of the most popular like Psalm 23 ("Lord's Prayer") or "Our Father."

Remember, it is about them, and not you. Spend time at your altar periodically and pray and sit with the Ancestors. Talk with them. You can also recite their names from time to time when you feel moved. Notice any messages, symbols, inspirations or ideas that may come to you during this time.

The spiritual part of our lives is our foundation and supports authentic health and well-being in every other area. Ancestor reverence connects us firmly with our spiritual roots in a way that is loving and nurturing. This allows us to understand ourselves within a more circumspect context. Ancestor reverence provides a pathway to healing familial wounds of past generations by strengthening the elevated Ancestors. They, in turn, can be in a better position to help those Ancestors who need it, as well as help you.

The ways in which we can attune to their "frequency" and have direct contact is by utilizing the modalities of prayer, ritual, altars/shrines, song, and dance. Ancestors are also able to visit their loved ones through dreams, visions and during meditations. Creating a ritual container for the Ancestors to depend on will make it easier for them to communicate when needed. This container will also serve as a space for communion with your Ancestors when you feel the need. Over time you will start to bring your Ancestors closer as well as become more keenly aware of their presence. It is important to build a relationship with the Ancestors. Your relationship must be nurtured like any other relationship. It takes time, patience, consistency and a strong intention to establish this very powerful spiritual alliance. Ancestral alignment will facilitate your coming to understand the power of non-physical reality and how accessing this realm can enhance healing at the deepest level.

Through consistent meditation, music, food and ceremony the bond between you and your Ancestral spirits will grow stronger and you will be able to communicate directly with them. Ancestral communication has been an ancient practice in every wisdom tradition throughout time. Your ability to connect with your Ancestors is always available. By creating your own personal shrine at home that you go and commune with your Ancestors, you are affirming your rights as a descendant and an inheritor of their unique legacy.

Ancestor Shrines at Family Gatherings

With growing interest in Ancestor reverence more and more families are including an altar setup at the family reunions, weddings, anniversaries and any other celebratory event. The altar is usually setup at the beginning of the event and stationed in an area where it will not be disturbed, but accessible so people can come and pay their respects, admire the pictures and reflect on their loved ones who have passed. Having an altar adds a special element of blessing to the event. Ancestor altars may also be found at spiritual retreats and other types of sleep away spiritual gatherings. Setting it up would be the same steps as if you were doing it at home. However, you must make it known to the Ancestors that this is temporary for them for this particular event.

Portable Altars

People move around frequently and miss the comfort and stability of their altars when traveling. As an answer to this, they are choosing the make a scaled down version of their altar with consecrated items ready to go in a box or other type of container. I don't see how this can work for Ancestors when it is about creating a "home" for them to dwell within your home. They are always with you as you travel around. I find this very interesting but If it works for you, then go for it.

Boveda:
Altar for Spiritual & Psychic Development

I include this special type of alter because some of our Ancestors are also our Spirit Guides. A Boveda table is a way to communicate and receive messages that are not only meant for you, but helps you develop your psychic skills in service to Spirit and your community. If that is a goal of yours, this altar would be a good one to setup. It can be in addition to your Ancestor altar, or some people combine the two. A Boveda table is a spiritual altar with a very specific configuration. One of the purposes of this particular type of altar is to strengthen your ability to connect to the Ancestral Spirits who act as your Spirit Guides. As a result of this practice, your intuition will become stronger and more clear. This particular style is from European spiritism of the early 1900s. This practice is very common in the Lucumi-Orisha and the Palo-Congo traditions as part of the spiritual development component for the devotees. Through this particular practice, each person is supported and encouraged to develop their psychic abilities. For those who are in service to the community as Spiritual Advisors, Priestesses, etc. this development tool is important to have in place. There are many, many, many versions.

Once established, it is a sacred space for those who wish to strengthen their connection and communication with their Spirit Guides by regular meditations at the altar. Once a strong connection to spirit guides has been established, insights will come about what to add or change on the altar. The altar is a fluid space which refuses to be stagnant. It is a creative process that develops and changes with time.

Traditionally, there are 1, 3, 7 or 9 glasses of water. Seven, being a very spiritual number and nine being the number associated with Ancestors/Egun. Seven and nine are the most commonly used number or classes. One of the glasses is much larger than the rest. It represents you. The remaining smaller glasses are placed in a circle with the largest glass in the center of the circle. The table should be covered with a white cloth. The center glass should have a crucifix or other spiritual representation (i.e. Ankh) large enough to lay across the top of the glass in the center. Also, include a white candle, flowers and any other objects that represent your spirituality on the table. It should be uncluttered and neat.

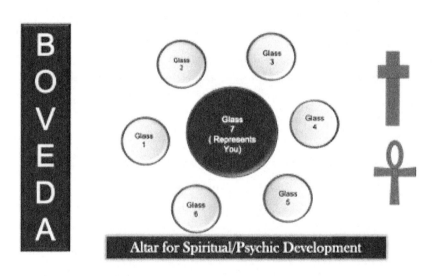

Altar for Spiritual/Psychic Development

Water is a powerful spiritual conduit that acts as a connecting element between the spirit realm and the physical realm. It also refreshes and cools which is the way you want to be and your spirits to be. The idea is to maintain coolness and replenishment of yourself and the spirits. Coolness is an ideal state as it is not too hot (agitating) or too cold (contracting.) Each of the smaller glasses is dedicated to a group of spirits that have been confirmed as part of your spirit lineage. Some practices dedicate the glasses in general to all of your Spirit Guides without getting into specific lineages. This altar becomes supercharged with energy as you begin to regularly connect with your Spirit Guides there. It becomes a portal, a sacred place to meditate, contemplate and pray and to convene with your Spirit Guides and elevated Ancestors. It is a creative and intuitive process.

Setting Up the Boveda Altar

The Boveda Altar is setup in much the same way as the Ancestor altar in terms of preparing the space. It should be setup on a tabletop. Ritual cleansing and purification of the objects and the space where you are setting up the altar is standard practice. Once you decide on how many glasses you would like to use (1, 3, 7 or 9.) Wash them and then cleanse them spiritually with a spiritual water you've made or that is readily available such as Florida Water, Kananga Water or Holy Water. Smudging is also acceptable as a cleansing. Repeat the same process with the ritual items (white cloth, cross/crucifix or Ankh, crystals, etc.)— anything else you will be placing on the altar.

After you've cleansed the area, table and all the objects that will be placed on the table, layout the white cloth and then begin to place the filled glasses of water. The largest one is first and goes in the center. Dedicate this glass to your highest spiritual guidance, development and evolution. Then place the rest in a circle around it going clockwise around. Dedicate each glass as you place it around to the enlightenment (light), evolution and guidance of your spirit Ancestral guides. Once you've place all the glasses, then place the crucifix, cross or ankh across the top of the glass in the center so that it rests on top of the glass. Place all your other items on the table. Take a moment and center yourself. Pray. Invite your guides to this table for them to help you connect with them and receive messages to help you and if you are to do work for others, to help others. Let them know whenever you sit there your purpose is to become spiritually grounded, stronger and more in connection with them and receptive to the messages they have. Take in the visual of this setup. This is representative of you being surrounded by the love, guidance and protection of your spirit guides. It also represents the spiritual flow and exchange that happens between you.

Change the glasses of water weekly. Should the water become cloudy change the water as soon as you can. Cloudy water signifies dense energy that needs to be cleared out between you and your Guides. Change out cloudy water as quickly as possible until it starts to remain clear for the week. Then go back to refreshing once a week. Having a Boveda is a commitment. Like any other altar it must be tended to regularly once you have set it up.

In some spiritual houses, the Boveda and Ancestor Altar are combined by placing pictures and representations of Ancestors on the Boveda altar. Or, some practitioners maintain both, but also put pictures of their Ancestors on the Boveda table. I keep mine completely separate. It is my belief that not all Ancestors are Guides. Most are for reverence and support. It keeps it simple.

How to "Work" Your Boveda

Dedicate a time daily, weekly or every few days to sit at your Boveda to meditate and connect with your Guides. Recite an opening prayer to begin the session and set a sacred tone. If your Spirit Guides like particular things such as a stone, shawl, skirt, drink, tobacco smoke, have it available so that if you get a strong inclination during your session, you have it right there with you. Getting up to get something after you've begun, interrupts the sacred container you have created. The reason to have the things that they like to do when they come to be near you is important in creating a strong connection with them. You get familiar with their ways of communicating and their subtle personality traits. Make sure to have a journal or a pad ready to write down messages. Set the mood with good smelling cleansing incense, splashing a spiritual cologne or essential oil around you, and lighting a candle, etc. If there is music that you like that sets the right mood for you to go within, play some of it during your session. Once seated, get calm, breath deep and relax. Once relaxed recite your opening prayer, a prayer of protection and begin to call out the groups of spirits that you have dedicated the glasses to and welcome them. You can use a statement such as, "I call on my Spirit Guides of my spiritual and ancestral lineages." You should always be extremely clear about this point. You only want the elevated spirits who come to help and uplift to be present. Also, be prepared to close out your session with "thanks to your Spirit Guides" and a closing prayer.

The three basic prayers to include in your Boveda session are:
1. Opening Prayer
2. Protection Prayer
3. Ask/Intent
4. Closing Prayer (giving thanks, releasing the spirits)

The 3 types of prayers mentioned above are standard. If you are someone inclined towards praying, feel free to add more prayers. They can be any that put you into a state of meditation and sacredness. Whatever prayers make you feel strongly connected to God and your Spirit Guides is appropriate for this practice. Praying from your heart is also just as good. The more sincerely and emotion, the more receptive you become and the stronger it calls to your Ancestors.

After you've finished your opening prayer and protection prayer, sit quietly and let the images and messages flow. If nothing happens, be patient. It takes time to develop the sensitivity and awareness to pick up the energies from your Spirit Guides. Often times, they begin to communicate right away, but it is you who are not yet skilled at recognizing the messages when they come. Don't dismiss something because you feel it is too small or insignificant. Building confidence is part of this process. Confidence is needed to further develop your psychic connection with your Spirit Guides. A level of trust between you is developed. We need to remain open and receptive to acknowledge and receive the messages. They will entrust us with more and begin to send in nore information and teachings. Be patient. It comes with practice, repetition and time. You have to learn the way they communicate with you and they have to learn the way you receive the messages best. It's a two-way conversation. You can also sit and just speak your desires for a strong connection to them also. Let them know you are ready to work with hem for evolution and development. Then be still and listen and/or see what they are trying to tell/show you.

Boveda Prayers

The following prayers are given as examples of how to pray at your Boveda. These prayers are for an actual bigger Misa that has multiple attendees, but you can modify them to suit your needs. These prayers have a non-denominational Christian emphasis which may or may not appeal to you. You can use any prayers that you have that are similar purposes – Praise, thanks, protection, ask, close/thanks. The prayers don't have to be anything long or drawn out. The simpler the better so that you will be more inclined to sit at your Boveda. Make the process comfortable and inviting.

OPENING PRAYER: I/We beseech You, O Lord God, the All Powerful, to send me/us the good Spirits to help me/us and take away all those who may induce me/us towards error; give me/us the necessary light so that I/we may distinguish truth from falsity.

Remove too, the maleficent Spirits, be they incarnate or discarnate, who may try to launch discord amongst me/us, and so turn me/us away from charity and love for our neighbors. If some of these Spirits try to enter my/our ambient, do not allow them access me/us.

Good Spirits, you see fit to come and teach me, make me yield to your counsel, turn me away from all thoughts of selfishness, pride, jealousy and envy. Inspire me/us to indulgence and benevolence towards our fellow beings, present or absent, friends or enemies; lastly, through the sentiments with which I am animated, make me practice. Your beneficial influence.

To (those) me as a Medium You chose as transmitter(s) of Your teaching, give awareness of the mandate and the seriousness of the act I am (they are) about to practice, so I/they may perform this act with the necessary fervor and meditation.

If I am (there be any persons present) driven by sentiments other than those of goodness, open my/their eyes to the light and forgive me/them Lord, as we forgive them, for any evil intentions I/they may harbor.

I ask especially that the Spirit of (INSERT NAME) who is my spiritual Guide, assist me and watch over me and my family.

PROTECTION: Beloved Spirits and Guardian Angels, who God in His infinite mercy has permitted to assist mankind, be my/our protectors during all life's tests! Give me/us the necessary strength, courage and resignation; inspire me/us towards all that is good, and restrain me/us from the downward incline to evil; may your sweet influences fill my/our soul(s); make me/us feel that a devoted friend is by my/our side, who can see my/our suffering and who participates in all my/our joys.

And you, my Good Angel, never abandon me because I need all of your protection to be able to support with faith and love the tests that God has sent me.

CLOSING PRAYER: I give thanks to the good Spirits who have come to communicate with me, and implore them to help me put into practice the instructions they have given, and also, that on leaving this ambient, they may help me to feel strengthened for the practice of goodness and love towards our fellow beings. Amen.

Ancestor Staff
(Opa Iku)

"Ancestors I call to you and invite you to a place on earth which is also your abode. A sacred grove I have prepared for you with love and adoration. When I hit my staff upon the ground let it reverberate out to the land of the Ancestors to let you know your children need you. Let our bond with Mother Earth, blood, bone and spirit warm your journey to your children. We await you."

In the Yoruba Orisha tradition of South West Nigeria and Lucumi of Cuba and the Caribbean, there is a custom of having an Ancestral staff (Opa Iku.) This staff is used as a further connection tool which allows you to call on the Ancestors in a powerful way. The staff is created by you. Energized by you. If at some point the Ancestors advise through divination for you to have your staff consecrated, this is done only by a Priestess/Priest, it will then become an Opa Iku. The required ceremony awakens the staff to its fullest power to communicate and interact with your Ancestral lineage. The Ancestral staff you make can be used once you've completed it. It will be effective just the way it is. Please note: It is recommended that you have a full Ancestor altar/shrine and have been developing your connection with them for a good while before you make an ancestral staff. The relationship comes first. Your comfort level in dealing with them is of primary importance. You don't want to "put the cart before the horse." A foundation of consistent Ancestor reverence practices has to be in place first. The staff is not a decorative piece. It is akin to a powerful amulet.

How to Make an Ancestor Staff

First, find a branch/stick in nature. A good time to find one is to go to the park or any place in nature after there has been a storm or it's been windy enough to knock branches from trees. Do NOT go out and find a tree and saw off any parts for your stick. It must be a stick that has already separated from the tree. Leave an offering in nature of a small amount of tobacco/and or sage, or corn meal at the place where you took the branch. An easier option is to purchase a plain wooden staff you can decorate. It is important it is natural wood. Not synthetic material. Ideally, it should be slightly taller than you, but if not possible at least past your waist. Something at least 2 inches in diameter or slightly more. Make sure it is easy to hold in one hand as it is a stick you will be working with. It doesn't have to be super straight, as long as it can act as a walking stick it should be fine. My staff reaches up to my eyes. I already had my branch prior to embarking on this spiritual journey. My family and I were in the habit of collecting branches from the park or driftwood from the ocean as nature objects to have around our home. When I decided to make my Ancestor staff, I immediately identified one of the driftwood branches as the one for my Ancestors. It had special meaning because my mother was the one who collected it. Once you have identified the branch, you will need the following:

- 9 different colored ribbons at least 20-30 inches long (but shorter than the stick.) Nine represents endings (Ancestors.) Any colors are good, however I made sure that I had black, white, red, green, yellow, and blue. There is no hard rule on the colors. It should be your intuition guiding the process. These ribbons represent the diversity of your ancestral lineage.
- 9 bells to tie on the end of the ribbons. Bells combine with the tapping sound are used to call the Ancestors.
- Herbal wash to consecrate the staff *(recipe provided)*
- Rum/Gin to spray and cleanse and "wake up" the staff
- Cigar to puff and create smoke to blow smoke on the staff for further cleansing and consecration. *(tobacco is very sacred)*
- Florida Water or sweet-smelling perfume to cleanse and attract uplifting energies
- Fresh cool water to keep the energy fresh and peaceful
- Palm Oil - for richness, wealth

- Honey, sweetness
- Votive or tea light candle (light)
- A bowl large enough to use as a catch-all
- Lots of newspaper or tarp to protect the work area.

Preparing the Staff

Prepare yourself mentally and energetically before you begin. Being in a slight trance is ideal so that you can receive messages easier from spirit as you work on your staff. Things may come to you from your Ancestor to do that is not included here. Close your eyes. Take a few deep breaths. Relax. Open your eyes. Light the candle. Get grounded. You can say a prayer of thanks or invocation if you like. If there is a type of music you like to play while doing spiritual work, put some on. Even better, you can make a playlist of music that keeps you in a spiritual mood and add some favorites of your Ancestors if you know of any. Some people, like me, are moved by African drumming. If you are, then add it to your playlist!

Herbal wash for Ancestor staff: Prepare the herbal wash. Take 2 cups of water and place into a saucepan and turn on medium flame. Wait until the water begins to boil and add: *Basil, Rue, Rosemary, Patchouli, Cinnamon stick, Chamomile, Anise, High John the Conqueror, dried Verbena.* Pray over the herbs and ask them to release their most potent energy into the water. Let simmer for a 5-10 minutes. Once finished, strain and let cool all the way. You can place the mixture in the refrigerator. Do not use the mixture hot. That will agitate the energy. You don't want that to happen.

There are fresh traditional herbs for this, but most people don't have access to them. They can be found in your local Botanica which is a store the sells spiritual supplies of a vast array, but particularly of the ATR's and Spiritualism. The dried herbs listed above are replacement herbs that most people can get. They are adequate. If you're near a Botanica and can get fresh herbs and know how to make a spiritual wash, the following herbs would be a better option:

- Rompe Saraguay (breaker/breaks up - to remove obstacles)
- Paraiso (paradise – blessings, happiness)
- Amansa Guapo (handsome, tame, good favor)
- Vence Batalla (win battles)
- Siguaraya (holy, sacred)
- Sauco Blanco (white swag, coolness)
- Verbena (verbena)

To prepare the fresh herbal wash: Rinse the herbs, take off the leaves of each one and place in a medium sized bowl of cool/cold water. Dispose of the stems in nature if possible, or the best way available to you. Once you have all the leaves in the bowl of water, begin to gently tear the leaves into the tiniest pieces you can over and over again until the water becomes green. Pray and ask the herbs to infuse the water with their most potent energy for the purpose at hand. Strain. The remaining pulp can be discarded or you can combine with the stems and boil them to extract more of the essence and strain and store the liquid in the refrigerator for a spiritual bath at another time. You can also make enough of the wash to take a spiritual bath for yourself. You can take it after you finish preparing your staff. This will add to your connection to your staff.

Preparation Steps

Clean the staff of all residue. Check-in with yourself and see if you like the stick just as it is or if you want to take of the top layer of wood. It's entirely up to you. If you do, this is the time to sand or shave it. Once that is done, rinse off the residue. Dry it. Now, you are ready to begin preparing your Ancestor staff. While you are preparing it, keep in the forefront of your mind the intentions of what you are doing (connecting with Ancestors from your mother's and father's side, all of the good elevated Ancestors, etc.) You can speak out loud to your Ancestors as you're preparing the staff. Speak of your hopes and dreams for yourself and for them and for building your relationship. Keep yourself psychically aware. You can gently blow your breath (which is an aspect of your ashe – divine energy) onto the staff. As you do this visualize your energy going to the staff and connecting. If you are angry or in a bad mood, reschedule doing this until a time when you are calm.

Ribbons: Tie the ribbons at the top of the staff so that they on. Some people wrap each ribbon a few times around the top and the tie it. Ribbons represent the diversity of your ancestral lineage

Bells: Add the bells to each end. Bells help in calling the Ancestors to you.

Next, place the staff in the bowl and hold with one hand as you sprinkle/pour the liquid items down the length of it.

Water: Begin to pour the water on the staff by holding the container at the top and allowing the water to cascade down the staff. Say *"fresh water, fresh water, refresh this staff so that it is perfect for my work with my Ancestors… keep them and myself with a cool head, cool attitude."*

Herbal bath: Repeat same action as water. Say, *"Spirits / wisdom of the herbs infuse my staff with your potent energies and qualities to make my staff empowered to do its work."*

Rum/Gin: Spritz along the staff, top, middle, bottom by filling your mouth with the liquor and spraying it directly on the staff. Say, *"Spirit water, wake up the essence of my staff so that it is ready to do its work with my ancestors.*

Cigar/tobacco: Puff (don't inhale) blow smoke all along the staff. Say, *"Sacred herb, awaken the staff to its sacred work with my Ancestors."*

Florida Water/Perfume: Sprinkle or spray along the staff. Say, *"Sweet aromas, attract all of my good and benevolent Ancestors to work with through my Ancestor staff and bring the same goodness to me and to my Ancestors."*

Palm oil: Rub from the top to bottom of the staff. Say, *"May the thick richness of the palm oil bring unending richness to myself and my Ancestors in the heavenly realm."* (have plenty of paper towels on-hand. This oil is very rich. Wipe of any excess. It stains. Be careful of clothing)

Honey: Rub from the top to bottom of the staff: Say, *May the sweetness of this honey attract all of the sweetness of life, joy, love, pleasure, abundance, wealth, success to myself and my Ancestors in the heavenly realm.*

Lay your staff on top of the paper/plastic covering on the floor. Leave the still burning candle next to it (always be fire safe.) Let it sit overnight. In the morning you can wipe of the excess oil & honey and sit it in the corner next to your Ancestor shrine. Present the staff to your Ancestors. Let it "marinate" in the energy of the ceremony for at least 3 days before you begin to use it.

Using Your Ancestor Staff

The Ancestor staff is used to call your Ancestors. You can do this daily, or when you provide a special feast or offering to them. Hold your staff in one hand and say an Ancestor prayer. Then recite each Ancestor's name with each tap repeating the name 3 times. This is to make sure they hear their name being called. (*Tap– Mabel Jackson, Tap– Mabel Jackson, Tap– Mabel Jackson*). The act of tapping the staff on the ground (earth) is creating a magnetic vibration which calls the Ancestors. The idea is the Ancestors are buried and their physical bodies have returned to the earth. You are calling on the DNA connection by tapping and creating this magnetic vibration.

General Offerings

After your altar and staff are in place, developing a schedule to build strong relationships is a practice that will bring great results. Determining a set day and time of day to sit at your altar, tap your Ancestor staff and just spend time with is one of the best ways to ensure connection with your Ancestors. I, personally, am not a routine type of person so I connect whenever I am inspired. Lighting candles and honoring your ancestors on their earthly birthdays and/or death dates and anniversaries makes them feel good.

Divination

Communicating with your Ancestors through divination is a common practice. They can advise you on your life questions, which direction to take in a given situation, tell you what offerings or actions they need from you to help them help you. Priestesses/Priestess of African Traditional Religions provide divination where the Ancestors can step forward and speak their advice. Also, there are specific Priests for Egun (Ancestors) who can do divination that is primarily for the Ancestors to speak. I recommend getting readings from a qualified and reputable Priestess if you want in-depth information. Divination is a resource that is invaluable.

There is a growing occurrence of people in the online spiritual community that have labeled themselves as Ancestor mediums. Mediums can be self-developed and not trained through a long line of Priestesses before them. I speak of those not initiated into a traditional system but operate solo and independently. Absolutely nothing wrong with it. However, all due respect to their great psychic ability to connect and deliver messages between Ancestors and their loved ones, however, a huge missing piece is the ability to divine what the "medicine" or "prescription" is to heal, remove obstacles and elevate your life. What good is information on problems without a remedy? On an emotional level, receiving messages from Ancestors is definitely wanted and can be healing to some degree by bringing closure. But Ancestral connection and alignment is a powerful spiritual tool that goes beyond messages. The time-honored practices of structured spirituality from ancient cultures is not to be dismissed as a way

to control and limit people. This is currently a popular misnomer that can turn people
away from much needed help and healing. Ancestral Divination is recommended at least once.

Writing A Petition to Your Ancestors

A petition is another way of communicating with your Ancestors. It is a ritual form of asking for their help. This practice is rooted in the Hoodoo tradition of the African descendants in southern United States. It is not as popular with those who follow the Ifa-Orisha tradition, although I have heard of a few people who use it as an additional step. A petition is a statement of desire(s) written in a specific way and usually on a certain type of paper. The paper is then folded in a ritual way and placed on the altar/shrine.

Parchment or brown paper is usually used. Parchment was used in ancient times to record magickal spells. It was known for being durable and lasting. Sometimes your petitions will stay on your altar for a long length of time and the more durable the paper, the better. Also, using parchment paper honors the old way of writing spells. Brown paper bag is a substitute both in durability and it is close to the color of parchment.

When writing a petition, be very specific and clear about what type of help you want and what it is you are asking for. It can be anything that is for your betterment. It is another form of conversation. In whichever way you would ask for specific, in detail is the way you would write it out. Once you're finished writing what you want, take a lit cigar and blow smoke on it to infuse it with sacred energy. The sacred smoke is said to carry prayers to the Spirits in heaven. Fold the paper to a quarter of the size. When you fold it, fold towards you once. Turn clockwise, fold towards you the second time. These motions represent pulling your requests to you. Hold it, pray over it. Then make the sign of the cross with the paper in hand and place it on your altar. The sign of the cross represents the crossroads, not Christ or the Christian cross. Whenever you are asking for help from the spirit realm you are doing it because you are at a crossroads of decision or action.

9 Herb Ancestor (Egun) Spiritual Bath

Taking a spiritual bath is a standard practice in African-based spirituality. Spiritual baths combine different herbs, oils, fruits and other natural items into water for specific energetic purposes. It's that simple. I have had spiritual baths made by others for me. Usually by a Priestess/Priest or Spiritualist. I've also made my own quite frequently. A spiritual bath is a great way to align yourself with various energies or to remove unwanted energies. In this instance the Ancestor spiritual bath is to strengthen the connection to one's Ancestors and open up your receptivity to messages from them. Life is filled with all kinds of distractions that take us away from our spiritual pursuits and keep us focused on the physical realm. When this happens, we can get so bogged down and blocked. This makes our energetic bodies too clogged or dense. It's hard to receive information from the spirit realm in this state. The bath I've included is provided with herbs that can be easily found in the grocery store or online. They are not traditional to any African spiritual practices, but have the energy needed to accomplish the goal of assisting in a stronger connection with your Ancestors.

- Basil
- Anise (star)
- Fresh tobacco (or a cigar opened up)
- Mugwort
- Clary Sage
- Lavender
- Parsley
- Rue
- Bay Leaves (1-2)
- **Additional ingredients**
- Petals of white flowers (any kind, but I like roses)
- Florida Water
- Essential oil of lavender

- Essential oil of Rose
- Essential oil of Lemon or Orange
- White candle
- Clear Quartz

Instructions: In a large pot fill with 3 quarts of water. Bring to a boil. Add the dried herbs. Strain into a large bowl. Add the essential oils. Put a clear quartz and lit white candle by the tub. Fill tub ½ way with warm water. Add the contents of the spiritual bath, petals, essential oils. Soak in the bath. Relax. Visualize negativity and heavy energies falling away from you. Say a cleansing affirmation or prayer.

An alternate method is to prepare the spiritual bath per the instructions but leave it in the bowl. Bathe or shower first. Remain in an empty tub/shower stall. Take the bowl with the bath. Say a cleansing prayer. Then pour the bath from your head and let it fall down your back and front. If your hair is a concern, you can pour the bath from the neck down (front and back.) Pat yourself dry.

You should feel refreshed after the bath. Meditation at your Ancestor or spiritual altar is recommended immediately after the bath. Repeating the bath for 3 consecutive nights would be advantageous.

Planetary Aids in Ancestor Communication:
Seasons, Planets, Eclipses, Retrogrades

There are times in the year when the veil between the earth and the spirit realm becomes thin. During this time accessing Ancestors and other spirits is easier. The most popular dates the veil is known to thin are on October 31st (Halloween), November 1st and 2nd (Dias de Los Muertos - Days of the Dead) and All Souls Day on November 2nd. *Halloween* comes from the Wiccan tradition of honoring the Ancestors and the Fall energy of nature receding into the earth to rest. *Dias de Los Muertos* is from Latin America which is the custom of honoring the deceased family members with dressings up as skeletons, feasts and ceremonies. *All Souls Day* is from Hoodoo tradition that specifically focuses on giving light and uplifting those deceased friends and family who have lived hard lives or died tragic deaths. Each tradition has its own way of expressing their how they honor the dead.

During those days is an advantageous time to commune with your Ancestors and pay homage. The thinning of the veil and the collective energy of intention of the Holidays provides a wonderful environment for contacting the astral realm. Meditating and calling on Ancestors for insight and protection during this time could yield strong results in communicating with them more effectively than at other times.

Planets
Certain planets resonate the type of energy for deeper Ancestor communication. Saturn, Pluto, and Uranus are planets that have these energetic qualities. When they are dominant at any particular time in the heavens, you can delve into communicating with your Ancestors.

Retrogrades
Retrogrades are when a planet appears to move backwards. It is an optical illusion. The planetary orbit appears to do so because of the relative positions of the planet and Earth and how they are moving around the Sun. This positioning modifies the energy of the planet that invites us to nurture and examine the qualities of that particular planet within ourselves. This turning inward or slowing down allows for us to feel the spirit realm. When this happens communication with our Ancestors is easier.

Eclipses
A solar eclipse is when moon passes between the sun and Earth. A lunar eclipse is when the Earth's shadow blocks the sun's light. Both phenomena

create a deeply ethereal energy across the entire planet. The ethereal energy is deeply conducive to the astral plane where the ancient Ancestors reside. Honoring the ancient Ancestors during these occurrences will allow for the opportunity for you to connect with them.

Ancient Ancestors who have escaped the wheel of incarnation are highly elevated. Certain energy frequencies around and within you have to be resonate specific vibrations for successful communication. Eclipses create a unique energy dynamic which supports connecting with Ancient Ancestors. Of course, you can try to connect with them at any time, but eclipse energy is extremely compatible to the realm in which the reside.

The following prayer I wrote inspired by an eclipse to connect with the Ancient Ancestral Mothers:

Ancient Ancestral Mothers Prayer

During this solar eclipse, today, I am calling my ancient of ancient mothers. The ones whose names have been lost through the eons of time. The ones who ascended long ago, ascended to their thrones in the stars. The watchers, the healers, the ones with magic in their blood and in their bones. The ones who never speak with their tongues because the power they emit is too strong for our ears to hear. They whisper their sacred message teachings with their eyes and their breath. Their love is so deep we named it a black hole because we forgot that was you sitting there in Immense unknowable unfathomable.
I miss you ancient mothers... when I think of you, I remember who I am ... that I am of you and we knew what I came to this earth to do
I call upon you ancient mothers whose names have been forgotten through the eons of time... at this eclipse when my spirit can once again perceive you and feel your love that satisfies my soul and gives me the fortitude to continue

*I welcome your whispered kiss and your celestial embrace. I need your
nurturing and medicine to heal these battle wounds
so that I can rise and be the daughter that you dreamed of,
Carrying the Soul Medicine out into the word.*
© 8/21/2017

7
Discovering Your Family Lineage

The Family Stories

The most easy and common way to discover your family lineage is through your elders and other family members. There's always that one or two people in the family who have an interest in the family history and have already collected and stored information. Oddly, the stories may seem familiar at a cellular level, connecting you to the echoes of all of our Ancestors. While your elders are still alive, get the history. Listen to the stories. The stories tell much about the time they lived and the era. Get the names (both legal and nicknames.) Record them on video or audio and save the digital file safely for future reference. Trust me, you will need it to go back to again and again. I recorded some of my elders before passing and unfortunately lost it due to changing my cell phone and not remembering I had the recording on it. So please save to a drive or cloud.

DNA Testing

Genetic ancestry testing is a way for people to go beyond what they can learn from relatives or from historical documentation. Examination of DNA variations can provide clues about where your Ancestors might have come from geographically. There are 3 types of this kind of genetic testing: Y chromosome, Mitochondrial (mtDNA), and single nucleotide polymorphism. Several companies offer DNA testing. The most popular are: AncestryDNA, 23andMe, African Ancestry (for those of African descent who want more detailed info), Family Tree DNA, and MyHeritage.

Getting DNA tests have become popular. What I love about them is that as an African American I can now know the specific people in Africa from which I have descended. It answers a lot of questions of why a person may

84

have certain affinities to different things in life. Don't only do the DNA test and get the results. Once you have the results, research the people. Go back into the most ancient times that you can find. Also, look at the society and culture from a global perspective. Compare what was going on in the rest of the world at various points in history. So much interesting things to find out!

Be sure to do your research about what DNA testing encompasses. When you get your DNA tested, you now have your DNA stored by these companies. If that is something that you don't want to happen, then that is a decision for you to make. It also would be important for you to be emotionally prepared for the results. You may uncover some history via your DNA you weren't aware of and are not happy about. Protect your emotions when doing a process such as this.

Adoption / Orphans

If you were orphaned or adopted and do not know your blood lineage, Ancestor reverence is still something you can incorporate into your spiritual life. Your Ancestors know who you are and will come when called. You replace reciting names with reciting "Elevated Ancestors from my mother's side, elevated Ancestors from my father's side." They will find ways to connect you with the information about them. If not, they will reveal themselves to you energetically over time. Also, those who were adopted and felt connected and loved by their adoptive family, they are also your familial line and you can honor them as your Ancestors too. The development of a strong loving bond throughout your life and as if you were blood family carries great meaning. It also builds a connection that is beyond the physical. All things that happen have a reason.

Ancient Ancestors

I have been asked previously about how to connect with your ancient Ancestors. This type of connection can happen. However, do not bypass your recent Ancestors. They are the link that gets you to the distant past. In contacting the Ancients who are elevated Beings and exist outside the wheel of incarnation, keep in mind that it will take time, persistence and consistency. They resonate energetically at such a higher and different vibration that their messages are harder to come through the veil to the physical plane. In order to make this connection easier, your personal spiritual development is key. When you are spiritually growing and developing it modifies your personal vibration. When this happens, it is easier to contact the higher planes where the Ancients are and receive messages, healings, teaches, etc. Do your part and they will do theirs.

Another way is to astral travel to the inner dimensions. Astral travel can take you to a higher plane when your own vibrational energy is a match. So, if you are involved in this practice, you can add an ancestral destination to meet your ancient Ancestors. This would be done in your prep work for Astral travel.

8

Incorporating Ancestral Reverence

Practices into Everyday Life

In Ancestral Reverence it is important for you to develop a routine that works for your lifestyle and schedule. Consistency is the only rule. Monthly, weekly and daily acknowledgements of your Ancestors help to create a very strong connection that enables growth and develop on both sides.

Greeting your Ancestor shrine/altar daily shows respect and honors them. It doesn't have to be anything big. A simple "greetings to all my Ancestors," will do. If you want to do something more significant, you can pour libation daily and you tap your ancestral staff in recognition of your Ancestors. Assign a day of the week that you do prayers or light a candle at the altar. You can also establish a part of the month you will do a bigger offering (flower, food, liquor, play their favorite music, auto-writing, etc.) New Moon, Full Moon or any of the other moon cycles can act as a calendar trigger to do your Ancestor ritual. Not necessary, but convenient and already established. Using yes/no divination to contact them and determine if you're in alignment weekly, monthly or every so often is another way to stay strongly in alignment. This is how I find out from my Ancestors if I'm in harmony (ire), and if not, what they need from me in order to be in harmony. I learned this from my Godfather in the Orisha tradition. Energy changes constantly and what was flowing a certain way one day can change the next day. Keeping in regular contact in this way ensures that they have what they need as quickly as possible to keep you supported in the right direction.

For example, my Godfather was visiting to check on my shrines and do other spiritual work. In talking with my Ancestors, he found out what they needed at that particular time. Through divination, he asked if there was something needed. He asked, "who needed it." He asked, "what was needed." I do this for myself as well. I ask the Ancestors if they would like the standard offerings. In addition, I listen for intuitive nudges as I am divining yes/no answers. Some of the other types of things that can come up as an offering are reading a particular bible passage, singing a particular song, playing music, reciting poetry changing around the altar, etc.

Ancestor reverence is fluid and you can be as creative as possible. Anyone that tries to keep you locked into rigid routine and rote rituals should be looked at again to see if they are right for you. If you're someone that needs that then stay with it. In my opinion it is more enjoyable when we can enjoy a free-flowing relationship with our Ancestors.

It is important to be respectful to yourself and your Ancestors and don't engage in things that would bring dishonor to the family. You definitely don't want to offend your Ancestors. When given messages or advice through divination, I suggest you complete what was given to you as soon as possible. If you were told to stop a certain behavior, do it as soon as possible. You see, when you decide to honor your Ancestors, it is a symbol of wanting to grow, develop, elevate and do right by them. If this is not your intention, then do not engage in Ancestor veneration.

9

Ancestral Last Rites the Ifa-Orisha Way:

Itutu Ceremony

The Itutu Ceremony is a traditional Yoruba last rite given to all deceased, not to be confused with the last rites given to deceased Orisha Priests of the same name. The word Yoruba word "itutu" translates to "refreshed." Although the name of both rites is the same, elements of the ceremony differ from non-initiate and Priest. The itutu is an involved last rites process with the urgent purpose of elevating the recently deceased to ensure their journey in the afterlife is smooth and successful. The understanding of the ancient Yoruba is that you cannot leave this to chance. It is important to take the necessary steps to support the spirit's journey. Not only is this about the individual who passed away, but it is also for the descendants so that they have a healthy and happy Ancestor supporting them from the ancestral realm. This is a relationship of reciprocity that supports well-being on all sides.

My Mother's Itutu Ceremony

When my mother passed away in 2005, we had a big memorial for her attended by family, friends and celebrities. She was well connected and known in certain circles. The memorial was a beautiful event. It involved performances dedicated to her by different artists, a few of them her children. Immediately following the memorial was a party filled with food, laughter, live music. Stories of her colorful life were shared. People who hadn't seen each other for many years were reunited under the celebration of her life. It was truly wonderful and the perfect way to honor her.

She was cremated and her ashes installed in the Wall of Honor at a Cemetery in Harlem, NYC. On the day of her internment, her children gathered privately to share more memories of her before we committed her ashes to rest.

Now that this had been done, as beautiful as it was, I felt compelled to ensure that her spirit got the most powerful and complete last rite. She was in a bad state prior to her death. She had multiple strokes and had gradually over many years descended into dementia. She had lost her ability to walk and take care of basic needs. Taking this into consideration, I knew that some of these debilitating ailments could follow her into the afterlife if she wasn't strong enough to shed them herself. It was my mission to ensure her spirit had what it needed to go to the non-physical realm totally released and lifted from that experience. I wasn't going to leave it by chance knowing there were specific rites performed by our Ancestors for thousands of years for just this purpose. My mother had always been my world. We were very close. She was close to all of her children. She had an uncanny ability to make us all feel loved equally. I was the last born. The baby. I took care of her for years when she fell ill. Just like I took care of her in life, I would do whatever it took to ensure she got the best support in her afterlife. I then sought for and arranged for the Itutu ceremony to ensure her spirit was lifted and strengthened on her journey to the land of the Ancestors.

I was fortunate at the time to know an Egungun (ancestral) Priest who offered to do the ceremony. He secured the ceremonial Bata drummers. These drummers have been trained in the ritual drumming for the Orisha and the Ancestors (Egun.) The drums are a central and important part to most any Orisha ceremony. Preparing for the Itutu took some time. There were several steps leading up to the day of the ceremony. Some of these certain steps involved meal preparation for the Ancestors, ritual feeding and washing and feeding of my Ancestor staff and adding personal items of my mother to it, like strips from her nightgown or other pieces of clothing that she used to wear. This elevated the Ancestor Staff to an Opa ku. Spiritual washing of the ritual items using specially prepared soaps infused with herbs was another step, and there were several other steps. The day of the Itutu arrived. The ceremony was taking place in my large apartment in Manhattan NYC. We moved some of the furniture out to make room for everybody. The apartment became packed as people arrived. Drumming, singing and dancing filled every corner of the apartment and circled in the air with excitement. Many of my friends and family were in attendance as well as other members and priests of the Orisha community. The apartment swelled with joyous drums, laughter, stories, and food. We sang the Oro Egun (nine songs to praise and move the Ancestors.) My mother's name was inserted at the appropriate part in the invocation, and we sang to her as an Egun (Ancestor.) The Itutu brings transformation, as the deceased moves from the world of the living to the world of the dead. The drummers had been setup in a large room that was her bedroom before she died. All the furniture had been cleared out of the center of the room. Everyone was singing and crowded around the drums. At one point in the ceremony when the drums reached a heightened pace and the voices of everyone singing rose to a crescendo, the energy in the room became electric. This is what happens when the spirits start to "come down." The space becomes filled with an "other worldly" feel. Portals open up. You can sense a shift that almost feels physical.

At this point, the two sconce lights on either side of one of the walls were turned on and the lightbulbs were lit. All of a sudden both lights started flickering. I was surprised because never in the 37 years our family had lived in the apartment had those lights ever flickered. They continued to flicker for a couple of minutes matching up with the intensity of the drumming and singing. At one point a Priestess walking across the room stopped in front of me and told me she saw my mother come into the room when the lights were flickering! My mother was called and had come to let us know she appreciated the sacred rites. The ceremony was a success.

It did what it was supposed to do. Ever since, the lights have never flickered again.

My mother continues to be a strong spiritual presence in my life and the lives of her children and grandchildren. She shows up frequently in readings, rituals and important initiations. She comes in our dreams, sometimes simultaneously. When we were in Cuba for my son's initiation to Shango, during the White Table Spiritual Mass that is customarily done prior to initiation to ensure that all his Ancestors were satisfied before he took this major step, she shows up. Immediately when the mass began and after all the prayers had been recited, the Spiritualist leading it looks at me and asks, "who is the lady that looks like you but is light-skinned?" That was my Mommy! My mother had come to give her blessings. The Priestess proceeded to relay messages from my mother to my son.

My mother, Anna Grayson, was a force of intelligence, beauty, elegance and creativity during her life. She was the epitome of motherhood. Late in her life she became very ill and debilitated. It was slow and painful. I believe the Itutu ceremony truly lifted her up out of the state she was in just prior to her death at a much quicker pace. It would have taken her spirit longer to shed the trauma of her earthly demise and come into full power as an elevated Ancestor. I was truly grateful to be in a position where I had the knowledge and resources to ensure my mother's spiritual needs were well taken care of.

10

Dispelling the Myths of Ancestor Reverence

Devil Worship?

There are so many misrepresentations of what happens in the afterlife. There is no absolute certainty around it. However, Hollywood has done a great job depicting Ancestors as spirits that come back to haunt and menace the living. This has greatly contributed to erroneous beliefs about the deceased. It undermines legitimate Ancestor Reverence. Hollywood in its depiction of spirits of deceased people in horror movies has severely maligned Ancestor reverence. As a result of this misrepresentation, Ancestor Reverence has been given a bad rap. It is also called "devil worship" by many in Christianity. This is far from any truth.

As a tool of terror of the slave trade in the United States, fear of death was driven into the enslaved Africans if they dared to practice any of their cultural systems. Slave owners knew that anything from their captives' cultures would empower and unify them. This was a tactic implemented by the power structure to help to ensure their dominance for hundreds of years. Even up until this day we differ greatly in how we worship the Divine. There continues to be a distinct polarization between those African descendants who have been heavily Christianized and those who have embraced their Ancestral traditions.

Elevated Ancestors are loving beings. They sacrificed in life for themselves and their families so that we are able to stand here today. They are fully invested in our continued survival. Even more so, they want us to achieve better than what they were able to do while alive. They want us safe, happy and stable. Descendants are the Ancestor's hope for the future. We are their hope and their continuation.

Summoning the Ancestors

In the spiritual arena, many people refer to their interaction with Ancestors in terms of "summoning" them. This is a huge error. The Ancestors are your deceased mother and father grandmothers and grandfathers, great grandmothers & fathers, great-great grandmothers & fathers, and aunties, uncles, etc. Imagine them being alive and you shouted to Grandma... "grandma, get over here I'm summoning you to help me with x-y-z..." What do you think her/his response would be? In Ancestor Reverence, you build connection, strengthen relationship, honor, respect, admire, ask, feed, welcome, embrace and raise up in prayer and light your Ancestors. There is no summoning involved. It is a relationship of family, love and reciprocity. Summoning is used in other spiritual practices to call upon low-level spirits to do your bidding. This is not done with your Ancestors.

Elevated Upon Death

One of the other misconceptions that is huge with Ancestor reverence is a person who was extremely dark, mean, negative, selfish, and lived a life that mistreated and hurt others is at once elevated when they die. That is not true. Upon crossing over how the person was in the life is how they are when recently departed. In some situations, they are actually more of what they were while living. The spirit plane is more vibrant and resonates more powerfully. However just like in life, each spirit is given an opportunity to evolve while in the ancestral realm. One of the important attributes of Ancestor Reverence is that every Ancestor benefits from the light and love that you send. This light and love will illuminate their path on the other side towards goodness. However, we do not include in our reverence the Ancestors who performed injustices and hurt us or others while they lived. There are specific rituals done for these Ancestors and are not part of core Ancestor reverence practices. Think about it... do you believe Hitler immediately elevated to goodness once he died? This type of Ancestor has to be dealt with differently than the rest.

Another misconception is that Ancestors are ghosts. This is far from the truth. Ghosts are spirits who have refused to move on to their spiritual journey and are stuck on earth because of it. They go about trying to experience this physical realm the way they were accustomed to in the life they just left. They can be a nuisance and troublesome to the living, especially if the living they encounter are not protected or too sensitive to the spiritual realm. They can also become attached to the living in some circumstances. They may also have unfinished business and deep regrets which may also keep them bound to the earth plane. There are special rituals and cleansings that can be done, should anyone encounter this type of spirit.

Ancestors are elevated beings who have willingly moved on to their place in the land of the Ancestors and claimed their seat at the foot of the Creator. They have, through their many incarnations, completed their assignments and elevated each and every time. They are part of the cycle of healing, love, light and spiritual evolution that is part of the Divine plan.

11

Christianity & Ancestor Reverence

"When one considers the phenomenon of ancestor worship it is clear that there is no comfortable fit with the Gospel. Protestant churches and the Roman Catholic Church have adopted different strategies to deal with this dilemma. Unfortunately, in some cases it has led to religious plurality and syncretism. "

Faculty of Theology
UNIVERSITY OF PRETORIA
PROF. P.J. VAN DER MERWE

In modern western societies honoring the Ancestors as the central part of religious practices has been nearly non-existent. In actuality, the concept of Ancestor reverence has been condemned as "devil worship," or "evil" by Christian authorities. Christians were made to believe that biblically Ancestor reverence had no validity and is far from the religious practices of any good Christian. In my observation, this sweeping proclamation is preached but not practiced.

What is interesting to note is that all of the most popular stories in the bible are about people who existed, lived and died before we were born. Ancestors. From the pulpit, congregations are preached the stories of the lives, trials and tribulations of these Ancestors in order to learn what to do and what not to do in accordance with divine law. These Ancestors are used as icons and examples of how to order our own lives. Jesus was born through the womb of a woman like the rest of us, lived, and died. He is an Ancestor that is worshipped, revered daily, weekly, monthly and yearly by Christians globally. As much as Christian theology tries to explain this away, it cannot be denied that Jesus was born from a woman and died. We are told that his spirit lives on and he will one day return. This is exactly what Ancestor reverence encompasses. Reincarnation. It is interesting to note that when it comes to Christian belief systems, you are expected to have a leap of faith without actual proof. When Christians view ancient belief systems that existed prior to Christianity, they dismiss them as superstition, because they say there is no proof. They also say that Ancestor reverence takes the focus away from God with earthly concerns for help and success. Quite to the contrary the tens of millions of people who have Ancestor reverence as part of their spirituality can attest to the help and healing the Ancestors bestow. They can also attest to how this spirituality has brought them closer to God by awakening the understanding of the endless continuation of life in a visceral way.

A friend of mine visited the Vatican as a devout Catholic who is also an Orisha Priestess. Upon her return she shared with me her discovery while visiting the Vatican. She observed that the Vatican exalted the Ancestors of the Knights of the Round Table through burying them underneath the Vatican! They are laid there to protect the Vatican as well. This is precisely what the Yoruba do to keep the ancestral energy close. Their Ancestors are buried beneath the compound where they live. Similar, do you think?

Whether knowingly, willingly, or not, Ancestor reverence cannot be avoided if you acknowledge that life didn't begin the moment you were born.

12

Prayers for Ancestral Reverence

Prayers are the soul of any type of worship and reverence. It is the language of the heart and mind focused on a particular spiritual goal. Saying prayers to uplift, call or ask things of your Ancestors should, without a doubt, be an integral part of your Ancestor reverence. Ancestors can understand all languages. However, different Ancestors in your family line may have a preference of language in which to speak or be spoken to. It is usually based upon the culture of their most recent or favorite incarnation. Ancestors who have escaped the wheel of reincarnation have retained the knowledge of their last experience on earth no matter how many thousands of years ago. It is usually their preference. Their language may not be known today, so you can speak with and to them with your preferred language. They will understand you.

Many times I have experienced Ancestral Mediums in a ceremony who become possessed by Ancestors, prefer to speak in the language they are most comfortable. Sometimes it's hard to get them to speak English, but eventually most of them do, or there is someone present who can translate. It is quite interesting to witness.

Think about who you are calling upon and what types of prayers and what language they would like to hear from you. Of course, if you are not able to speak in a foreign tongue, your native language is adequate. Also, the style of prayer may also be important for your Ancestors. For instance, if your Ancestors were Christians, Muslim, Jewish or East Indian they might prefer to hear invocations from the Bible, Koran, Torah, or Bhagava Gita, respectively. It is important to consider this before automatically settling on English or Yoruba. Sensitivity, awareness and flexibility is to be applied.

The following given prayers are in either English or Yoruba, also with Yoruba/English translations:

Morning Ancestral Prayer

Now that I am waking up,
I give respect to the realm of the Ancestors.
Let all good things come to me.
'Inner Spirit' give me life.
I shall never die.
Let all good things come to me.
Let it be so.

Prayer to My Ancestors

I salute all my Ancestors of my bloodline who sit at the feet of Olodumare, Chief of the Heavenly world.
I pay homage to all the generations that meet generations in Heaven.
I call on all my Ancestors in-order-to remember and honor you. I ask for guidance and protection in-order-to break the cycle of negativity which stifles my spirituality.
I ask for your blessings and assistance as I develop to be a person of good character.
I pay homage to the spirit of the Ancestors.
I pay homage to the spirit of cool water.
Bring me the power to pray to the Ancestors.
Bring me blessings of Peace and Longevity.
Bring me blessings of Good Fortune.
Bring me the blessings of Calmness.
Bring me the blessings of a Stable Home.
Bring me the blessings of Dependable Transportation.
Bring me the blessings of a loving and Compatible Wife/Husband.
Bring me the blessings of Good and Obedient Children that will make me proud and uphold the legacy.

Bring me the blessings of spiritual Guidance.
I cannot live or die without my Ancestors.
I thank the water for its many blessings.
I pledge never to knowingly offend my Ancestors,
So that shame and envy would be no more,
Negativity and loss would be no more,
Tragedy is no more,
To be overwhelmed is no more,
Disrespect is no more,
Sickness is no more,
Disease is no more,
Curse is no more,
Witchcraft is no more,
Court case, litigation and fight are no more,
Death is no more.
Only immortality.
That only Good things and Abundance may come to me,
And, also, to my family and to all the good people of the Universe.
I am a person of good character.
I ask for composure, caution, patience, understanding, deep thought,
uprightness, longevity, health, fortitude, wealth, prosperity, love,
happiness, teach-ability, endurance, strength, power, flexibility, wisdom
and all good things.
Mojuba Olodumare, Mojuba Olodumare, Mojuba Olodumare
Egun, Egun, Egun lead me home.
Ase, Ase, Ase!

Praise to the Ancestors
I give praise to the universe
I give praise to mother earth
I give praise to all of nature and its beings
I give praise to all my guiding spirits
I give praise to my Ancestors
I give praise to all that came before me in this struggle
I give praise to my elders
I give praise to all those who have cared for me, protected me, guided me and loved me
I give praise to... (add any others you wish to give praise to)
(End with Ashe or So Be It)

Yoruba Oriki (Praise Poem)
E nle oo rami o.
I am greeting you my friends.
Be ekolo ba juba ile a lanu.
If the earth worm pays homage to the earth the earth always gives it access.
Omode ki ijuba ki iba pa a.
A child who pays homage never suffers the consequences.
Egun mo ki e o.
Ancestors I greet you.
Egun mo ki e o ike eye.
Ancestors I greet you with respect.
Ohun ti wo ba njhe lajule Orun.
Whatever good things are being eaten in the realm of the Ancestors,
No mo ba won je.
Eat my offering with them.
J'epo a t'ayie sola n'igbale.
Eat richly from the earth.
Omo a t'ayie sola n-igbale.
The children of the earth are grateful for your blessing.

Ori Egun, mo dupe.
I thank the wisdom of the Ancestors.
Ase.
May it be so.

In phonetic Yoruba
A in-lay rah-mi oh
Bee a-kow-low bah jew-bah e-lay ah lah-knew
Oh-moh-day key e-jew-bah key e-bah pah ah.
A-goon mo key ee oh.
A-goon mo key ee oh e-kay a-yeah
Oh-hun tee who bah jay-ee la-jew-lay Oh-ruin
Knee moh bay wow-un jay
J-eh-po lie-yeah oh
Oh-moh a t-ah-yeah show-la eg-bah-lay
Oh-re A-goon moh dew-pew.
Ah-shay

Oriki *(praise)* to Egun *(Ancestors)*

Egungun kiki egungun.
Praise the Ancestors.
Egun iku ranran fe awo ku opipi.
Ancestors who have preserved the mysteries of featherless flight.
O da so bo fun le wo.
You create words of reverence and power.
Egun iku bata bango egun de.
On the strong mat you spread your power.
Bi aba f'atori na le egun a se de.
The Ancestors are here.
Ase.
May it be so.

Smudging & Cleansing Prayer
Use to cleanse your altar space energetically with incense or spirit waters

Creator, Great Mystery (God, Olodumare)
Source of all knowing and comfort,
Cleanse this space of all negativity.
Open our pathways to peace and understanding.
Love and light fills each of us and our sacred space.
Our work here shall be beautiful and meaningful.
Banish all energies that would mean us harm.
Our eternal gratitude.

After setting up your altar you can do a prayer something like this:

"This is your child (state your name), daughter/son of (state your mother's name) and (state your father's name). I have created and blessed this space as a portal for you to visit and dwell in my home. I welcome you and give honor and give light to you. I call those Ancestors who are elevated and sit at the feet of God. I call my Ancestors who dwell in light, love, and positivity to come into this space. Thank you for your blessings and assistance. Ashe, ashe, ashe."

13

My Ancestor Work

I am called to further this important work in ways that help spread the medicine of the Ancestors. In my work, I've helped people connect with Ancestors who they knew in life as well as Ancestors from generations ago in their family line. The wisdom and the love that they have been able to receive and give has given them a deeper sense of spiritual connection and grounding. In another instance, I helped connect a participant in my workshop with their Ancestors. As a result of this connection, they are helping an Ancestor work to contribute positively in this timeline to heal in the past where that Ancestor had done some not so good things when they were alive. This is important healing of an ancestral wound that will, in turn, unhook the family from the pain that Ancestor caused during their life. The Ancestors are sending messages of healing and love and want to help us elevate to our next best expression of the Divine.

I am an ordained Interspiritual Indigenous Faith Minister with emphasis on serving those who are interested, pursuing or involved in ancient indigenous spiritual cultures. I can assist those who are interested in beginning on their path of Ancestor Reverence. Please feel free to reach out to me with any questions at the.rev.mignon@gmail.com or on Facebook you can find our group, Sacred Mysteries World Wide. Sign-up for our blog at: www.sacredmysteries.org/blog

14

Conclusion

Becoming in alignment with your Ancestors, is becoming alignment with the legacy of your spiritual DNA. The strength of the love the Ancestors provide is the type of nurturance that makes us feel more supported and not so alone. WE can better relate to our past and our family histories and become better able to grasp our destinies within a holistic viewpoint. Decoding from the inside the knowledge and wisdom that may not otherwise be available to us, or be a long time coming. The Ancestors can help us access this information more readily.

Ancestors give us an advantage. They do not have the physical barriers that we have and can traverse the inner spiritual world to obtain information and strategies necessary for success and then give us access when we call on them. Whether it be through divination, dreams, mediums, visions, meditations, etc. they make sure we are constantly looked after, cared for and supported. The level and strength of the support they can provide is dependent upon how we develop our relationships, build our energetic ties in the form of offerings and sacrifices that will build stronger and stronger pathways.

Our relationship with our Ancestors not only helps us during our lives, but also when it is time for us to depart our lives. They are there to welcome us and ease us of the shock of departing the earthly world. They also act as our guides and help us become reacclimated to our spiritual bodies and the noncorporeal world.

My daughter was only 5 years old when my mother passed. My mother was very ill when my daughter became aware of her. She was homebound and then eventually bedbound. My daughter only new of her this way. She never saw her dressed in regular clothes, only her nightgowns. After my mother passed, my daughter since has always let me know when her grandmother comes to visit her. She visited often not long after her passing. My daughter describes to me when she sees her grandmother in the spirit realm and what my mother is doing, what she is wearing and what is going on with the rest of the family too. Her descriptions are extremely accurate in their depiction of the way and how my mother would be dressed and would spend her time. She described her relaxing on the beach, reading a newspaper, wearing a Kaftan, enjoying the ocean, and the sun somewhere on a tropical island. This is my mother's most favorite past time. My daughter's visions of my mother bring her a type of peace that she doesn't get anywhere else. It is a special connection the reaches across dimensions.

Finding out more and more of your family history, legacy and ancestry will reveal patterns, inheritances, and talents that you would otherwise not have known. This informs you of who you are, at what part you on and how you need to grow and/or continue along your path and destiny.

We are here today because of those who have come before. We benefit from their survival, accomplishments, advancements, ingenuity, love and devotion. Our survival is dependent upon the useful and valuable legacy inherited from them that will be of benefit for generations to come. The mysteries of life they could not uncover during their lifetime have been left to us to unravel with their blessings from the Ancestral realm. Our Ancestors advanced their societies the best way that they could and left us signs, symbols and blueprints to guide us with added prayers that we continue to do the same for our descendants. During their lives they called on their Ancestors which nurtured the continuance of the spiritual connection from generation to generation. We are the descendants they dreamed of. They are us and we are them returned in the endless cycle of life. We have within us the spiritual and physical DNA which connects us through time and space. Honoring them is honoring ourselves and those that will come in the future.

It is my hope that this work will help those who wish to start or further develop their Ancestral veneration and pay homage to the legacy that they come from. The legacy is much more than a few generations ago. The legacy spans thousands of years back into antiquity. Ancestors reverence opens up the ability to access ancient and recent legacies to help guide and heal. This is truly a gift to hold with deep gratitude and love. A journey to embark upon with love and joy.

15

Ancestor Reverence FAQs

The following are a list of FAQs that I have come across in my area of Ancestral work.

1. ***Can I give offerings to relative who recently passed away?***
   No. It is recommended to wait and give them time to get adjusted to being in the land of the Ancestors. You can light a candle to light their path. Then after a few months check to see if it is time to add the Ancestor to the shrine and give offerings.

2. ***What if I'm adopted can I still participate in Ancestor reverence?***
   Ancestor reverence encompasses both your blood family and your adoptive family. If you don't know your blood family include them as "Ancestors from my mother's side, Ancestors from my father's side." They know who you are.

3. ***What if I'm an orphan?***
   The same as if you were adopted. Please see #2.

4. ***Can you give your ancestors anything you want?***
   Preferably, you give them what they want. If you don't know, then give them what you have and they will accept it.

5. ***What if you don't know their names?***
   Recite their names as "Ancestors from my mother's side, Ancestors from my father's side.) They know who you are.

6. ***What do you do with the food afterwards***
   If this is an offering prescribed through a reading then it should be determined at the reading how long to leave the offering and what to do with it afterward. If this is an offering you initiated yourself,

then you can leave it for them overnight and dispose in the garbage or in nature. It can stay longer if you feel it should.

7. **How do you know which Ancestors are the right ones to venerate?**
   If you don't know the Ancestors, leave them out when you recite their names. Asking for your "elevated Ancestors' to be present will only call to those that mean you good. The benevolent Ancestors.

8. **How do you know what they like and don't like?**
   Family stories and what you remember about them. Ask around. Otherwise, divination is another way to find out what they like or want to receive from you.

9. **What is Ancestor money? Why do you use it?**
   Ancestor money is from Ancestor reverence in parts of Asia. It is not a Yoruba Orisha practice. People are adopting it without knowing its origins or the particulars of how it was used in Asian spirituality. I always ask my Ancestors if they want something, especially if it is a different or unusual practice to my Ancestral ways.

10. **What if the Ancestor I am trying to reach reincarnated already?**
    When an Ancestral spirit reincarnates, there is an aspect of them that remains in the land of the Ancestors from their previous incarnation. You will still be able to reach the Ancestor that you would like to. Spirit is vast and linear and manifests multitudes of forms in multitudes of realities and dimensions.

11. **What if your Ancestors were heavy Christians? Can you still revere them in this way.**
    If the Ancestor is elevated, they will appreciate that you remember them and the gifts you send them regardless of their religious beliefs. Good energy is good energy.

12. What's the difference between bad Ancestors vs people who were strict?

Ancestors who are troublesome were troublesome in life. They had bad character which affected the well-being of others and the community in a negatively impactful way. They were harmful. An Ancestor that was just rude, obnoxious, strict, or argumentive, doesn't put them in the category of a "bad" Ancestor.

13. Should I include my spouse's family members on my Ancestors' altar, especially if we have kids together?

I would do separate altars. If space is an issue, one large altar with Ancestors on either side if you know they would get along. The children will have more to love and experience with two Ancestor altars.

14. Can I pray to someone else's Ancestors to help them?

No. You can pray to your Ancestors to seek out their Ancestors to alert them to help the individual. You are your Ancestors' responsibility. They don't mind giving messages to someone else's Ancestors. However, if someone is a Spiritual Practitioner that has been initiated and/or anointed to spiritual work for others, they may be able to ask their Ancestors that help them in their spiritual work to assist someone else.

15. Can I honor my Ancestors without an Altar?

Yes. All you need are prayers at first. Your prayers can be your altar until you are able to set one up. Also, you can light a white candle and set a glass of water next to it. Dedicate the candle and water to your Ancestors. Say "light and progress to all my benevolent Ancestors." If you have names, you can say them.

About the Author

Mignon Grayson is the founder of Sacred Mysteries World Wide and an ordained Interspiritual Indigenous Faith Minister with an emphasis on Indigenous Faith, Traditions & Religion. She is affiliated with One Spirit Interfaith Seminary in New York City. Ordained in 2016, she chose the interspiritual path due to her calling to serve people of all faiths and spiritual practices. Mignon recognizes that there is a common link to the Divine Creator within all faiths, spiritualities and religious traditions.

She is a devotee of the Ifa Orisha tradition of Nigeria and initiated as a Yayi (Priestess) in Palo Mayombe, which is rooted in Congo spiritual tradition. As a result of her spiritual journey, Mignon has learned the deep importance of the Ancestors and their connection to our daily life and our spiritual evolution. This is a theme throughout most ancient cultures. Mignon's particular focus is to bring the wisdom of ancient spiritual traditions from across the world to the masses through Sacred Mysteries World Wide an online and in-person learning hub.

As a spiritual mentor and evolutionary coach, Mignon seeks to inspire and support people on their spiritual journey by assisting them in connecting with their most authentic and sacred soul expression. As a sound healer, Mignon uses the vibrational energies of sound to bring about healing by energy recalibration. She works passionately to be a constant vessel of healing, love and spirituality. She can be reached at the.rev.mignon@gmail.com

Links

Sign-up to be notified about our events & classes
www.sacredmysteries.org/signup

Contact the author directly at:
the.rev.mignon@gmail.com

Follow us on Instagram @sacredmysteries_ww
https://www.instagram.com/sacredmysteries_ww/

Checkout the blog at our website:
www.sacredmysteries.org/blog

Join our Facebook Group:
https://www.facebook.com/groups/789238771271870

We Are Always Here to Help
Just getting started on your spiritual path? Click the link below to our YouTube channel which has videos that can help you on your journey:

YOUTUBE

Sacred Mysteries World Wide YouTube Channel:
https://www.youtube.com/channel/UCpgEudpK0Rhs3KaPii7ZIaw

ANCESTORS! How to Honor, Connect & Setup an Altar
https://youtu.be/PKKxv8-h3JY

How to Create Ancestor Altar *SIMPLE & EASY*
https://youtu.be/IVWJI7HQMBc

Guided Ancestor Meditation - Build A Stronger Connection to Receive Their Guidance
https://youtu.be/S3Ht0ek_sZ8

SOURCES

Dreams & Ancestor Visits
https://www.feedspot.com/?hash=feed/fof_fo_1317615__f_83975/article/6495719503?dd=4311523274496373

Ancestor Money - Joss Paper
https://en.wikipedia.org/wiki/Joss_paper

Boveda Prayers: Allan Kardec Prayers
https://kardecist.org/spiritism/prayers/spiritist-meetings/

Printed in Great Britain
by Amazon

37620459R00066